SAPPHO:
POEMS & FRAGMENTS

SAPPHO

POEMS
& FRAGMENTS

TRANSLATED WITH
AN INTRODUCTION BY

JOSEPHINE BALMER

BLOODAXE BOOKS

ISBN: 978 1 78037 457 4

Second, expanded edition published in 2018 by
Bloodaxe Books Ltd,
Eastburn,
South Park,
Hexham,
Northumberland NE46 1BS.

www.bloodaxebooks.com
For further information about Bloodaxe titles
please visit our website and join our mailing list
or write to the above address for a catalogue.

Supported using public funding by
**ARTS COUNCIL
ENGLAND**

Digital reprint of the 2018 second edition.

Contents

ACKNOWLEDGEMENTS

Sappho: Poems & Fragments was first published by Brilliance Books in 1984. In 1996 Bloodaxe Books published a revised and corrected edition, for which Josephine Balmer re-wrote much of the introductory material and corrected and altered her translations of the poems. This was reprinted in 1999 and 2014.

This second, expanded edition (2018) includes Josephine Balmer's translations of eight recently discovered fragments not included in the previous editions along with a new essay, 'The New Fragments: Texts, Translations and Retranslations'.

INTRODUCTION

Sappho and her Critics

> After his nephew had sung one of Sappho's songs over the wine, Solon
> of Athens, the son of Execestides, told the lad to teach it to him immed-
> iately. When someone asked why he was so eager, Solon replied, 'So
> that I may die knowing it.'[1]

Solon's instantaneous and uncomplicated delight in Sappho's poetry
typifies the attitude of the Ancient Greeks to her work. She was
considered one of their finest poets, an integral part of their cul-
tural history. Her face was engraved on coinage, her statue erected,
her portrait painted on vases. Many ancient commentators praised
her literary genius, while Plato, among others, called her 'the tenth
Muse'.[2]

For the modern reader Sappho's poetry can be far more difficult.
Over the centuries much of her work has been lost and those poems
which have survived are fragmentary – a few lines quoted in pass-
ing by later writers or pieced together from scraps of papyri exca-
vated in Egypt. Often there is little indication of the context of the
piece, of what precedes or follows. Greek literary traditions can
also be alienating; the composition and performance of poetry was
very different as, more importantly, were its social function and
the expectations of its audience.

The greatest problem Sappho's poetry presents is its eroticism
– a problem because so many translators and commentators have
found it so. Sappho's reputation has changed since Solon's time;
today her name is synonymous with 'unnatural sexual relations
between women', as the *OED* puts it, rather than artistic excellence.
Many studies of her work are preoccupied with her sexuality, with
discussing whether she was 'morally pure' or a 'disturbed pervert',
whether she was merely inclined towards 'inversion' or whether
she practised it as well.

The feminist scholar Mary Lefkowitz has pointed out that these
biographical obsessions are typical of the critical treatment of
women writers.[3] In literary mythology, male genius derives from

an overpowering urge to create, a devotion which surpasses the mundane claims of the material world and triumphs admirably over superfluous domestic ties. Female genius, on the other hand, evolves as compensation for the lack of a 'normal' domestic life – the correct outlet for women's creativity. Hence Virginia Woolf is frigid, Emily Dickinson is a frustrated spinster, Charlotte Brontë is disappointed in love and throughout history Sappho has been physically repellent (i.e. unable to attract a sexual partner), promiscuous and passionately jealous.

Because women's creativity has been so directly linked to the circumstances of their lives, their work is often regarded as autobiographical; an emotional outpouring which is divorced from literary artifice and intellectual precision. One scholar, for example, has written that Sappho's poetry has the 'air of reality, of being derived immediately and directly from Sappho's own experience'. Similarly, in a discussion of No.32 (94*LP*) in which Sappho describes the parting dialogue of two separated lovers, he comments: 'it is not hard to believe that some conversation took place and that its substance was not entirely different from this record of it.'[4]

These comments and many like them appear to praise Sappho's work but in fact deny the strength of her poetic imagination, denigrate the artistry and subtlety of her work and ignore the importance of inherited literary and social convention. They are typical of a great many commentators who consistently project on to the text contemporary male assumptions about the nature of women's art. A more balanced assessment, as some classical scholars are beginning to argue,[5] should attempt to discard prejudices, while acknowledging the difficulties of interpretation and appreciation. It is necessary to place Sappho in her historical context, to examine the importance of her gender and sexuality and to ask what was the nature of her genius and the extent of her achievement.

Sappho and Greece

Despite the many theories, claims and counter-claims, very little is known about Sappho's life. Evidence is slight and, as is so often the case with classical history, most of the details are tentative. The main difficulty is that the oldest surviving biographical accounts were written several centuries after Sappho's death and the longest, an entry in the *Suda*, an historical and literary encyclopaedia, was written in the tenth century A.D. Piecing together all the available facts, historians agree that Sappho lived *c.*600 B.C. on the island of Lesbos, in the eastern Aegean sea off the coast of Asia Minor (modern Turkey), probably in Mytilene, its largest city. Beyond this little else can be substantiated. Most of the sources give details about Sappho's family – parents, brothers, husband, daughter – but these cannot be proved. Her poetry mentions a daughter, Cleis, an unnamed mother and brother and it can only be assumed that these are her own. The lifestyle described in her poems suggests that she was a member of the wealthy, ruling aristocracy and this is reflected in the sources.

What sort of society did Sappho live in? In the *Iliad* and the *Odyssey*, the epic poems attributed to Homer and completed about 700 B.C., an aristocratic warrior class exercises complete control. Its wealth is based on land and its society is grouped around the extended family, the *oikos*, who live on rural estates. By 600 B.C. the basis of power was the city state, the *polis*, where the aristocracy still clung to a tenuous control. Greek civilisation was in a period of transition, caught between the demise of the old ruling class and the rise of a new political system and consciousness, democracy. Rival family factions struggled for power and, in many cities, tyrants seized control.

Lesbos, and Mytilene in particular, were not immune to these troubles. The aristocracy still held power but they were a class in crisis. In the late seventh century B.C., the ruling tribe or family in Mytilene was the Penthilidae, who misused their power and clubbed their opponents to death in the street. When they were overthrown, feuding aristocratic families fought for control. The exact sequence of events is unclear and the evidence is confused. To complicate matters, from *c.*610 B.C. Lesbos was involved in a war with Athenian colonists at Sigeum, near Troy on the coast of Asia Minor.

There is some evidence that Sappho was involved in this turmoil. Around 600 B.C. the family faction of the aristocratic male poet

Alcaeus attempted to overthrow the current regime of the tyrant Myrsilus. But his fellow conspirator, Pittacus, went over to Myrsilus's camp, betrayed his companions and Alcaeus's faction was expelled. Sources note that Sappho was a contemporary of Alcaeus and Pittacus and one states that she was exiled to Sicily.[6] In her poetry she mentions some of the rival groups; the Penthilidae in No.46 (71 *LP*); the Polyanactidae in Nos. 45 (155 *LP*) and 99*LP* and in No.74 (98b*LP*) the Cleanactidae. The fragmentary text of 98 also contains the word 'exile' or 'flight', although the rest of the sentence is lost and its meaning is obscure. In the poem, Sappho laments the fact that she is unable to provide her daughter with a headband from Sardis. The context of this statement may well be that Sappho is in exile and unable to obtain the luxuries of Lesbos but it is impossible to prove this conclusively.[7] What is important is that these references show that Sappho was aware of, if not involved in, contemporary political events.

One important consideration is the position of women in this period and the way in which they were affected by social changes. Aristocratic society in Lesbos was similar to that described in the Homeric epics. Fundamental to this patriarchal and militaristic culture was a sharp division between male and female activities, a delineation of their separate roles and spheres of influence. Government, trade, but mainly war were the business of men, and glory in battle their greatest achievement. Women, often the spoils or prizes of combat, were excluded from political or economic activity. Their purpose was marriage, their glory, chastity, their world, the home. 'Go home and attend to your work, to your loom and spindle,' Hector tells his wife, Andromache, in the *Iliad*, 'and see that the woman servants attend to theirs – war is the concern of men.'[8] Outside the home, religion was the only public activity in which women could participate. They supervised the cults of the female deities such as Aphrodite, Hera and Artemis and it is therefore not surprising that these figure prominently in Sappho's poetry.

Despite this role division, the evidence of Homer's poems suggests that women were less restricted than they were a few centuries later. They appear to mix freely with men, they are present at public feasts and their opinion is often sought and respected.[9] In the *Odyssey*, Odysseus prepares to visit his father. 'My house and my belongings,' he tells his wife Penelope, 'I leave in your care.'[10] In a society in which tribal and family ties were politically important, marriage was considered desirable and a bride was respected, if only for her family connections.[11] Many commentators believe that women were particularly valued and esteemed on Lesbos.[12] To a certain extent this might be true: Sappho, at the very least, had some knowledge of political events, she was certainly educated and her poems illustrate that men and women were not totally segregated on Lesbos.

Yet the old world was vanishing. The individual warrior, for example, was being replaced by soldiers in group formation, the *phalanx*. This had a far-reaching effect on aristocratic society which was gradually transformed from a military into a leisured class.[13] Male culture remained deeply competitive but the emphasis turned from war to athletics and sport. Men began to congregate at the gymnasium and wrestling-ground and the symposium, a male drinking party, became the focus for political and social life. These changes led to an increased segregation of the sexes and the seclusion of women inside the house.

On a wider scale, the structure of society was changing, from large rural estates to the smaller households in the city state, from the extended tribal groups to self-contained nuclear families. Women were valued less and less for their family connections or for the political alliance their marriage might cement. Instead their position within their husband's family became important as well as their ability to provide sons for the inheritance of property and citizenship from which they were themselves excluded. Marriage began to be seen as a burden to men and women's sexuality thought dangerous and alarming.[14] The philosopher Solon, for example, who lived in Athens in the early sixth century B.C., was reputed to have said that a man should try to have sex with his wife at least three times a month.[15] An explicit misogyny, absent from Homer, appears in later poets. Hesiod, who wrote epic poetry at the beginning of the seventh century B.C., tells the story of Pandora's box, attributing the presence of evil in the world to women, 'a bane to mortal men'. Semonides of Amorgos wrote a long invective against women in the mid-seventh century, comparing them to various unpleasant species of animals.[16]

This devaluation of women is reflected in changing attitudes to the mythical heroine, Helen of Troy. In the *Iliad*, war breaks out between Greece and Troy when Paris, a prince of Troy, steals Helen from her husband, Menelaus of Sparta. Later Greek writers found it impossible to believe that a ten-year war could be fought for the sake of a woman.[17] Significantly, Helen was an important image for Sappho who uniquely invests her with autonomous thought and action. Whether women on Lesbos were valued or not in Sappho's lifetime, it was still a society in crisis. And the outcome of this turmoil, as we have seen, brought fundamental ideological and social changes for women. It therefore seems reasonable to expect Sappho's poetry to contain responses to these changes and to reflect the increasing tension between the sexes.

Sappho and Sexuality

A few centuries after her death, Sappho's name began to be surrounded by scandal. Faced with the anomaly of a woman poet, many commentators reported that she was a prostitute, while others told apocryphal stories about her unrequited love for a ferryman, Phaon, and her subsequent suicide.[18] Much of this information originated in comic plays about Sappho written and produced at Athens in the fourth century B.C., although only a few scattered references survive.[19] These comedies probably made biographical assumptions about the eroticism of Sappho's poetry and may well have been used as a source of information by later biographers. A papyrus fragment from the second or third century A.D., for example, claims that 'some people accused' Sappho of being 'a lover of women'. Porphyrion, writing in the third century A.D., comments that Sappho was called 'masculine' either because of her poetic skill or because of her homosexuality. The entry in the *Suda* states that she had a reputation

14

for 'shameful liaisons with women'.[20]

But the fascination for salacious details really began at Rome in the first century A.D. with the Latin poets Horace and Ovid. In Ovid's famous poem, the 'Epistle of Sappho and Phaon', later translated by Alexander Pope, Sappho relates how she once loved Anactoria, Atthis and all the other women mentioned in her poems but now she has rejected her 'shameful' past for the love of a man, Phaon: 'what once belonged to many women,' she tells him, 'now you alone possess'.[21] The concept of vicious forbidden love, of shame and guilt and the rejection of a deviant lifestyle for a man who does not love her all became standard features of the mythology of Sappho.

This image was adopted in particular by nineteenth-century French writers, obsessed by decadent sexuality. In Baudelaire's poem 'Lesbos', Sappho indulges in lurid frenzied relationships with women until she is overcome by her passion for Phaon. Verlaine's poem 'Sappho' follows a similar pattern. Pierre Louÿs' semi-pornographic work, *Les Chansons de Bilitis*, appeared in 1895 and contained the familiar description of life on Lesbos; Bilitis, a newcomer to the island, is seduced on arrival by Sappho. Gradually, through the work of these and other writers, Sappho had become a sexual rather than a literary celebrity.

Classical scholars were horrified by these portraits of Sappho. One, Wilamowitz, was so outraged by Louÿs' inferences in particular that he immediately rushed to Sappho's defence. In his book, *Sappho und Simonides*, published in 1913, he repudiated all claims that Sappho was a sexual deviant. Instead, he said, she was a wife and mother, a paragon of womanly virtues. He noticed that a few ancient commentators referred to the women in Sappho's poetry as her 'pupils' and claimed that she was the leader of a formal cult at Lesbos, dedicated to the worship of Aphrodite. The women in her poems were young initiates whose literary and moral education she supervised. But his sources were highly suspect; the main piece of evidence, a comment by Maximus of Tyre that Sappho's relationship with the women in her poems was similar to the philosopher/ teacher Socrates' relationship with his male following, is extremely ambiguous.[22]

Although Wilamowitz's views are no longer fashionable, some modern scholars are still influenced by them. C.M. Bowra, for example, in his book *Greek Lyric Poetry* (1961) writes that it is wrong to compare Sappho's poetry to that of the male homosexual poets, although 'in later times...Sappho's emotions were misjudged and hard names were given to her'.[23] Judith Hallett, in a recent article in *Signs*, claims that Sappho held a 'formal' position at Lesbos which she links to the segregation of the sexes. She denies Sappho's lesbianism and sees her as a 'sensual consciousness raiser' whose poetry is a 'social vehicle for imparting sensual awareness and sexual self-esteem to women on the threshold of marriage and maturity'.

In general, recent commentators concede that many of Sappho's poems are passionate expressions of love between women. Yet most scholars are still worried about the nature of this passion. Albin Lesky, for example, states that Sappho's love is a 'desire for spiritual domination' and that 'there is nothing to suggest that it had any base origin'. Denys Page comments that Sappho's poetry displays 'a lover's passion' as well as 'an overwhelming emotion of the intensest love' but concludes that there is no evidence to suggest 'practice as well as inclination'. The anthropologist George Devereux takes this discussion a stage further. He decides that Sappho was a 'masculine lesbian' with a 'clinically commonplace female castration complex'.[24]

The application of these theories to Sappho's text results in some strange readings of her poetry. No.20 (31*LP*), in particular, has been subjected to some unusual interpretations. Wilamowitz, faced with such sensual writing, explained that it was a wedding song performed at the marriage of Sappho's favourite pupil. 'That man' is the bridegroom and Sappho's emotion is sorrow at being parted from the girl. Page refutes this theory but, like many other male scholars, sees the man as the focus of interest. Sappho, he claims, feels passionate jealousy towards the man who is favoured by the woman she loves.[25]

George Devereux cites the poem as evidence of Sappho's homosexuality which he sees as a pathological condition. She is not jealous of the man, he writes, because she cannot help but identify with his masculinity. She finds him 'equal to the gods' because he has something which she cannot offer the woman – it is all a simple case of phallus envy. Devereux concludes that Sappho's emotions affect her so violently because her 'girlfriend is taken away from her not by another lesbian but by a *man* who has what she does not have and what she would give her life to have'.[26]

In search of evidence to support their theories, scholars scour Sappho's poems for references which could be construed as conclusive either way. Judith Hallett, attempting to prove that Sappho was exclusively heterosexual, notes that she had a daughter (No.75 [132*LP*]), while others point to No.41 (121*LP*) in which marriage with a younger man is discussed. For the other side, four lines are presented which are said to contain explicit proof of physical contact: No.4 (46*LP*), No.12 (126*LP*), No.32 *l.*22 (94*LP*) and No.47 (213*LP*). One fragment, which seems to include the word *olisbos*, the Greek word for a leather phallus, has been adopted as evidence by both camps (99*LP*).

But the real difficulty is not the evidence but attitudes towards it. Sappho's poems are not autobiographical tracts and should not be treated as such. First there is the consideration of poetic persona, of the subtle and complex use of 'I' in poetry. The transformation of experience into art is rarely straightforward and although Sappho's own voice is certainly representative of personal feelings, it is also governed by literary conventions and by the intentions of her poetry. There is also the practical problem. It is impossible to ascertain the context of many fragments, especially the shorter pieces; they might well be part of reported speech or dialogue as in Nos 39 (137*LP*), 78 (1*LP*) and 61 (109*LP*), for example, or even from an account of a mythological story as in Nos. 97 (142*LP*) and 88 (54*LP*).[27]

Scholars who attempt to "explain" or classify Sappho's eroticism in pedantic, clinical terms refer only to contemporary thought. But what was the attitude of the Greeks and how was it reflected in Sappho's poetry? As we have seen, segregation and a sharp division of sexual roles led to women's sexuality becoming an object of fear for Greek men. Women were thought to have a larger sexual appetite than men and heterosexual sex was thought to strip men of their virility.[28] The story of Actaeon, who was torn to pieces by his own hounds when he caught sight of the goddess Artemis bathing, illustrates the strong taboo against female nudity.[29] In the seventh and sixth centuries B.C., votive statues of young men, *kouroi*, depicted nude figures, whereas those of women, *korai*, were clothed.[30] Historians link increased segregation, the growing exclusiveness of male culture and the emphasis on male prowess in war, with male homosexuality and concede that in aristocratic Greek society it was considered not only acceptable but desirable; the male rather than the female form was thought to be the embodiment of beauty, love between men, the romantic ideal.[31]

It is also often inferred that aristocratic Greek women, neglected and despised before and after marriage, imitated male society and turned to their own sex for physical gratification, almost as a last resort.[32] Certainly, as well as Sappho's poetry, there is other evidence which refers to love between women and some which links it with Lesbos. The male poet Anacreon who lived on the mainland of Asia Minor in the sixth century B.C., describes how the woman he loves ignores him because 'she is from Lesbos and gapes after another woman'.[33] An early sixth-century plate from Thera and an Attic red figure vase *c.*500 B.C. show women 'courting'[34] and arousing each other. An epitaph from Athens dating from the late fifth century B.C. also records the love of two women:

> Because of the truth and sweetness of your love,
> your companion, Euthylla, placed this stone
> on your grave, Biote; she remembers you
> forever in her tears and weeps for the youth
> you have lost.[35]

Perhaps the most important reference to female homosexuality is in Plato's *Symposium*, written in the early fourth century B.C. At a drinking party each guest is called on to make a speech about love. The comic playwright Aristophanes relates a spurious myth to explain sexual longing; once people were double beings but when they angered the gods, they were split in two. Now they long to be complete again. Those who were once a man and a woman seek each other out, as do those who were once two men and those who were once two women; for it is only in the sexual act that they can temporarily regain their wholeness.[36] Plato's attitude is singularly

18

lacking in moral judgement; to him, sexual preference was merely a matter of chance.

Sappho's work has a similar shamelessness and lack of self-consciousness. Her poetry is sensual and emotional rather than sexually explicit. The erotic intensity of her work is well illustrated by No.32 (94*LP*), in which she describes a parting from, and memory of, a loved companion. All attention is centred on the absent woman and, in particular, on her body: Sappho tells us that her friend sat by her side; that she wove garlands around her neck – in vase painting a common feature of homosexual courtship; that she anointed herself, which was usually done while naked after a bath; and finally that she satisfied her desire. The description of their surroundings is also imbued with sensuality: the various flowers; the rich perfume; the soft bed; the stream. Sappho heightens the emotional strength of the poem by creating an imaginary world of memory, occupied only by herself and her lost lover.[37] In the context of this coherent poetic focus it seems trite and redundant to ask whether 'the girls of Lesbos…sought to induce orgasms in one another by bodily contact'.[38] Rather more important is the internal poetic meaning of Sappho's sensuality and exclusive concern for women.

In male Greek poetry, desire for women is expressed in vague terms. Romantic intensity is reserved for relationships between men. These are traditionally described in terms of military combat, as a hopelessly imbalanced struggle for domination with one partner, the *eromenos* or loved one, inexorably running away from the other, the *erastes* or lover. Some scholars claim that Sappho's erotic concentration on women illustrates the transference of dominant male values to the world of women.[39] But this view represents a fundamental misunderstanding of her poetic intentions. No.78 (1*LP*), for example, in which Aphrodite is summoned for help in a love affair, certainly echoes male conventions; Sappho calls Aphrodite her *summachos*, her ally in battle, and begs her not to allow her heart to be subjugated or conquered. In the sixth stanza, in particular, flight, pursuit and the giving of gifts are all elements of formalised male relationships.[40] Yet in Sappho's poems, this exchange is not static; roles will be reversed, beloved will soon be lover and vice versa.

Love between women is not a matter of domination and subordination – their desire is mutual and equal.[41] Using the framework of male literary conventions, Sappho creates an alternative world in which a set of female values are asserted in direct opposition to those expressed in male culture. In this poetic world, desire between women, sensuality and an appreciation of female beauty do not represent an imitation or transference but a rejection of male values and a response to the increasing devaluation of women and fear of their sexuality.

Sappho and Poetry

After asking, 'Is Sappho fit to read?' J.A.Davison, like many other critics, turns to consider the question, 'Is she worth reading?' Although most scholars eventually answer in the affirmative, a brief survey of their comments suggests that it is a close-run thing. Denys Page, for example, writes that No.33 (96*LP*) is 'devoid of anything profound in thought or emotion or memorable in language'. Most believe that Sappho's poetry derives directly from her own experience and therefore decide that her language is 'simple' or 'homely', her style, 'unadorned with literary artifice'. Often, we are told, her emotion proves stronger than her art; she is carried away by a flight of fancy, an irrelevant train of thought or an unsuitable image. Alternatively, it is said that she uses conventional settings – a farewell speech or a prayer – as a backcloth for a descriptive piece with no ulterior poetic design.[42]

Most of these scholars ignore the difficulties involved in appreciating Sappho's poetry. To begin with, sixth-century Greece was an oral culture and poetry was performed to an audience. Furthermore, it was not spoken but sung or recited to musical accompaniment. This convention created its own needs such as the repetition of key words, a fluency of thought, a logical movement of expression and a powerful climax, all of which can be found in No.78 (1*LP*), the prayer to Aphrodite, Sappho's only complete surviving poem.

Similarly, the lyric form, used by Sappho and her contemporaries, was still in its infancy. Earlier Greek poetry, the *Iliad* and the *Odyssey* for example, had been epic. But in the seventh century a new type of poetry emerged, the lyric, which was short, personal and spoke directly to its audience about individual emotions. There were different kinds of lyric, including the choral, sung by a choir at a formal ceremony, such as a religious festival or wedding, and the monodic, favoured by Sappho, which was sung by a single voice and was more personal in subject matter. The youth and freshness of the lyric genre should always be considered in any judgement of Sappho's work. In No.112 (34*LP*), for example, she calls the moon 'silver', which is an extremely ordinary analogy by modern standards, common in the popular literature of romance. Yet ancient commentators praise Sappho for this comparison and record that she was the first to use it. This point might seem obvious in studies of, say, Shakespeare, many of whose metaphors have become part of everyday speech, but has often been overlooked in those of Greek poetry.

Another problem is that little is known about the performance of Sappho's poetry. Some scholars believe that all of her poems were designed to be presented at a cult ceremony while others argue that she performed them privately on informal occasions. Scholars also dispute whether her audience consisted of both men and women or whether they were exclusively female. The only reference in Sappho's extant work to the performance of her poetry is No.98 (160*LP*), which seems to suggest that at least some of her poems were sung to a private audience of her women companions. Her marriage songs were obviously performed at weddings, some by a choir. There is also evidence that some of the fragments had their origins in cultic worship, particularly No.95 (140a*LP*) in which young women are invited to mourn the death of Adonis, the beautiful young lover of Aphrodite whose worship had arrived in Lesbos from the East. All in all, it seems reasonable to suppose that Sappho's poetry served not one but a variety of purposes.

Finally there is the question of Sappho's position as a woman poet. A.R. Burn has commented that Sappho appears to take this for granted and argues that on Lesbos in particular, but elsewhere in Greece as well, poetry was a common pursuit of women.[43] There are references in Sappho's poetry to the poetic skill of her friends; in No.22 (22LP), for example, she invites Gongyla to 'take up your lyre and sing for us' and here, as in many other fragments, the practice of poetry is linked with desire. The ancient sources contain information about several women poets from other parts of Greece, some of whose poetry still survives. But even in antiquity their work was often denigrated. Praxilla, who lived in Sicyon in the fifth century B.C., was famous for the silliness of her poetry. There is also a story which tells how Corinna, who is also thought to have lived in the fifth century, defeated the male poet Pindar in several poetry competitions, although her victory is imputed not to her poetic skill but to her outstanding beauty which is said to have swayed the judges.[44] A surviving fragment of Corinna's verse scolds another woman poet, Myrtis, for competing with Pindar, 'although she is only a woman' and this illustrates that women writers themselves felt far from confident about their work.[45]

The first charge made against Sappho's work by modern scholars is that her language and style are prosaic and simplistic. She records events as they are, as they have happened to her, it is said, and makes no attempt to display an artistic discernment. No.33 (96LP), for example, has been the subject of many criticisms. Scholars are worried by the central image of the poem which compares a woman absent in Sardis to the moon and extends the simile to include a description of the natural world over which the moonlight falls. Some critics believe that the moon and woman are mutually identified; as the moon sheds its light over the sea and fields, so does the woman.[46] Others argue that, instead, the moon and the woman are contrasted; the calm of the moon is placed in opposition to the restless grief of the absent lover.[47]

But most commentators see the image and subsequent description as a literary red herring. Denys Page writes that the moon begins as a symbol of the woman's beauty but rapidly becomes nothing more than a charming digression which has little to do with the rest of the poem.[48] Richard Jenkyns also adopts this attitude and believes that Sappho's account is nothing more than a catalogue of names.[49] Such comments fail to grasp the essence of Sappho's art.

Her images cannot be decoded or exchanged for another single meaning nor do her descriptive passages focus on objects at random. Instead she is concerned with a wholeness, with a unity of expression. In No.33, the extended simile exhibits an overall richness, a sense of ripeness and weight which is echoed in each of the objects mentioned; the sea is filled with salt, the fields with flowers; the dew moistens the earth and the blossom blooms. This impression links the woman with the natural world for her heart also is 'heavy with grief'.

Many scholars have been puzzled by Sappho's use of the epithet 'rose-fingered' to describe the moon in this poem. Homer applied the phrase to the dawn and this has been interpreted as a reference to the red light which streaks across the sky as the sun rises. Some critics claim that Sappho's description must mean there is a 'rosy glow' around the moon and most assume that rose equals red in colour.[50] But it makes far more sense to assume that Sappho refers to a white rose, to the white light of the moon. This is reflected in the remainder of the simile, for each of the other elements of the night are also white in colour; stars, salt, dew and flowers – roses, chervil (cow parsley) and honey-clover (white meliot).

Again these images connect Sappho's description of the moon-lit night with the woman in Sardis. Ancient commentators report that Sappho loved the rose and used it in her poetry to express her appreciation of female beauty.[51] In Ancient Greece this was often associated with pale skin; on vases, for example, women's bodies were painted in white. Through the image of the rose, the woman, the moon, the flowers and night are mutually associated. Sappho further identifies the woman with the natural world by interweaving some of her favourite descriptive adjectives, usually applied to her companions, between the two; the chervil, for example, is 'delicate', the woman's heart, 'tender' and the dew, 'beautiful'.

A similar unity may be found in No.79 (2LP) in which Aphrodite is summoned to her sacred temple and grove on Lesbos. Here Sappho is concerned with creating a sense of atmosphere; the grove she describes is not necessarily a real place at any given time but an imaginary paradise which reflects and contains Sappho's vision of Aphrodite. The season – spring; the garden setting; the apples – a symbol of fertility and Aphrodite's own fruit; the flowers – again roses; the horses; the soft breezes and the drowsiness are all highly erotic. The description is also extremely sensual, containing references to sight, touch (the breezes and the cups), sound (the murmuring streams and rustling leaves), smell (the burning frankincense and the blossom) and taste (the nectar).[52] But Sappho is concerned with the spiritual as well as the sensual. Each exotic element of the grove echoes the cult of the goddess it houses. Through the strength of Sappho's imagery, the place of worship and the experience of worship become inseparable. Sappho's poetic skill here and elsewhere lies in a strict control of subject, a tension between language and emotion and a resonance of image. Her powerful and direct style might well be 'simple' but in its simplicity it is also extremely sophisticated.

Sappho and Women

The subject and themes of Sappho's poetry have been criticised in much the same way as her language and style. Modern scholars report rather scathingly that her poems are mostly concerned with the minutiae of daily existence, with 'trivia', 'tittle-tattle' and 'back-biting'. Denys Page, for example, writes that her principal themes are the 'ephemeral pleasures and pains of an idle but graceful society'. He points to a 'narrow limitation of interests' and claims that more serious matters than those discussed in her poetry must be left to 'more reflective minds on graver occasions'.[53]

As ever, belief in the autobiographical nature of Sappho's poetry prejudices appreciation of her work; critics claim that in her poems she is 'bitchy' or 'gossipy', that the women she 'sneers at' are leaders of rival associations or friends who have deserted her group for another. In this context, the lines 'I do not have a spiteful temper/ but a tender heart' (No.10 [120LP]) have been quoted with irony. Scholars also note that Sappho is excessively concerned with the fripperies of fashion. Albin Lesky writes that in No.72 (44LP),

Sappho 'betrays' her 'female heart' by her description of Andromache's dowry. Again, in a discussion of No.74 (see above, page 9), Lesky states that Sappho's juxtaposition of 'the politics of her menfolk' with her interest in fashionable headgear, 'delightfully illustrates her exclusive and immediate concern with the feminine'.[54]

In one sense, Lesky is correct – Sappho is exclusively concerned with the world of women, with their everyday life and occupations; 'mother, dear', she writes in No.40 (102LP), 'I cannot weave my cloth'. Many of her poems describe religious cults which, as we have seen, were important to women – their only opportunity to participate in public life. But Lesky's comments, intended to expose Sappho's frivolity, serve only to trivialise the intentions of her work. They illustrate a bias against women's art, a contempt for women's experience and a firm belief that there are more suitable subjects for serious literature. Sappho's poems do contain references to clothing (see No.22 [22LP], No.24 [100LP] and No.25 [39LP]) but these are not fashion bulletins. Instead, Sappho draws attention to women's clothing and hence their bodies as an expression of her sensual appreciation of female beauty. Again, in No.74, her purpose is not to discuss the availability and purchase of headbands but to portray the relationships of mothers and daughters over three generations.

Another poem which celebrates love between mother and daughter has been described by Richard Jenkyns as 'charming but slight'.[55]

> I have a beautiful daughter, golden
> like a flower, my beloved Cleis,
> for her, in her place, I would not accept
> the whole of Lydia, nor lovely... (No.75 [132LP])

But far from being 'slight' this small fragment expresses one of the main concerns of Sappho's poetry. To the inhabitants of Lesbos, the kingdom of Lydia, their neighbour on the mainland of Asia Minor, represented wealth, power and luxury. It was a country with extensive natural resources and was also a centre for trade. During Sappho's lifetime, Alyattes, the Lydian king, extended its frontiers by military conquest and began to amass a vast personal fortune. Sappho's rejection of Lydia for Cleis represents a preference for the experience of women over the male world of politics, trade and war. The image appears again in No.21 (16*LP*); for Sappho, beauty rests in the sight of Anactoria's face rather than Lydian chariots and so it is Anactoria she loves and values, desire between women she asserts over the male concept of military glory.[56]

The poems which Sappho wrote for performance at wedding ceremonies also illustrate her concern with women's experience. As we have seen, marriage was considered a woman's sole purpose, the height of her achievement, but gradually her role within it became devalued. In the work of male poets such as Semonides and Hesiod, wives are characterised as shrewish, lazy, greedy and promiscuous. The only positive advantages of 'acquiring' a wife were the heirs she might bear and the work she would do, providing she was carefully trained and her disposition proved suitably malleable.[57] In Sappho's wedding songs emphasis is laid on the qualities of the bride and the good fortune of the groom. In No.63 (113*LP*), she tells the groom that 'no woman was ever lovelier' than his bride. In addition, men in her poems are eager for marriage; in No.62 (112*LP*), the groom has 'prayed' for his marriage and 'dreamed' of his bride. Sappho understood the significance of marriage for women. She re-affirms their importance within the marriage partnership, the value of their contribution and characterises relations between husband and wife in terms of mutual love and respect, not fear and hatred.

Linked to Sappho's poems on love and marriage are those concerned with virginity. In Greek society, chastity was a symbol of female honour and some of Sappho's poems reflect this: 'I will remain a virgin/for ever,' she writes in No.70 (152*E*). But society also insisted that women should marry and have children, that their virginity should be surrendered:

> [Why am I unhappy?]
> Am I still longing
> > for my lost virginity?   (No.69 [107LP])

Sappho stresses the physical trauma of loss of virginity but more importantly her poems symbolise the emotional trauma of marriage and its effect on women's lives – the separation from family and friends and the move from their own home to the strange surroundings of their husband's house and family.[58]

A poem by Alcaeus, Sappho's male contemporary, describes the marriage of the mythical Peleus and Thetis: 'he took her from the halls of Nereus to the home of Chiron; he unclasped the pure virgin's girdle and the love between Peleus and the best of Nereus' daughters was consummated.'[59] Thetis's role is passive. She is not even mentioned by name but identified only by her chastity and by her father's name. In comparison, Sappho's poetry is startling; by focusing entirely on the reactions of women to virginity and its loss, on their sense of honour, their distress and sorrow, she animates their experiences and takes them far beyond the dumb, shadowy figures of Alcaeus.

Another interesting point of comparison between Alcaeus's poem and Sappho's work is their contrasting attitudes to Helen of Troy. Alcaeus compares the 'wicked deeds' of Helen, which, he believes, were responsible for the destruction of Troy, to the virtue of Thetis who remained faithful to her husband and whose son, Achilles, was instrumental in the downfall of the city. Alcaeus's view is derived from Homer; in the *Iliad*, Helen is blamed for the war between Greece and Troy and is shunned and despised by many Trojans. Furthermore, she voices her own shame at her elopement with Paris, calling herself 'evil-minded and detestable'. In one passage she weeps as she remembers her home and the family, parents, husband and daughter she has left behind.[60]

Sappho makes no moral judgement on Helen. In No.21 (16*LP*) she asks the question 'what is the loveliest sight on earth?' and answers that it is subjective – 'whatever you desire'. Helen is cited as an example to prove the point. Sappho dismisses Homer's claim that Helen was ashamed of her actions and longed to go home and defiantly tells us, echoing Homer's exact words, that Helen forgot all the ties which bound her to Sparta. In Homer, Helen is passive; she is first abducted by Paris, lives in misery in Troy and is finally reclaimed by the victorious Greeks as a prize of war. Sappho's Helen has a will of her own. She is not stolen like an inanimate object but deliberately leaves Sparta and sails away to Troy. Paris is not even mentioned. Helen is no longer a puppet of kings but a woman who makes her own decisions, who desires and acts on that desire, forsaking her traditional role as daughter, wife and mother. For these reasons, Page duBois has described this poem as 'one of the few texts which breaks the silence of women in antiquity, an instant in which women become more than the object of men's desire'.[61]

Sappho does not reject or even criticise the accepted place of women within her society. But the tension between male and female experience implicit in her poems reflects the changing status of women. In reality this tension was resolved by the devaluation of women and a restriction of their freedom. Sappho's poetry creates an alternative world in which aspects of women's lives are celebrated and a preference for their concerns is expressed. This preoccupation with women, which has troubled so many scholars, is unique in classical literature. Far from a source of weakness, it is closely linked to Sappho's poetic achievement, to her passionate sensuality, her exploration of beauty and desire and her concentration on the emotions of the lover, all of which had a profound influence on subsequent literature. At least the Greeks were in no doubt:

> Wherever you are, lady, equal of the gods, greetings;
> for we still have your immortal daughters, your songs.[62]

Notes

Abbreviations used in Introduction and Notes:

LP = Edgar Lobel et Denys Page (eds.): *Poetarum Lesbiorum Fragmenta* (Oxford, 1955, repr. 1963).

E = J.M. Edmonds (ed.): *Lyra Graeca Vol. 1*, Loeb Classical Library (London, 1928).

PMG = *Poetae Melici Graeci*, ed. Denys Page (Oxford, 1962).

1 Aelian, quoted by Stobaeus, *Anthology* 3.29.58.
2 *Palatine Anthology* 9.506.
3 'Critical Stereotypes and the Poetry of Sappho', Lefkowitz, pp.59-68.
4 Bowra, pp.187, 192.
5 See especially McEvilley and 'Advice on How to Read Sappho', Lefkowitz, pp.69-70.
6 *Suda* iv 322s; Eusebius, *Chronicle* 01.45.1; Strabo 13.2.3; *Parian Marble* Ep.36.
7 See Page, p.102, note on *ll.*7-9.
8 *Iliad* 6.490-92.
9 In the *Odyssey*, Odysseus and Nausicaa converse freely (6.110-315), although Nausicaa is worried that her reputation will be damaged if she is seen with a strange man. She also advises Odysseus to supplicate himself before her mother, Queen Arete, rather than her father, King Alcinous, because her opinion is influential (6.310-15).
10 *Odyssey* 23.355.
11 See Pomeroy, p. 34, who cites Herodotus's account of the competition for the hand in marriage of Agariste, the daughter of Cleisthenes, tyrant of Sicyon, 600-570 B.C. (Herodotus 6.126-31).
12 See J.A.Symonds, quoted by Page, pp.140-2; Pomeroy, p.55; Bowra, p.178.
13 See Murray, pp.192-208.
14 Hesiod, *Theogony* 603-12.
15 Plutarch, *Life of Solon* 20.3.
16 Hesiod, *Works and Days* 54-105; *Theogony* 567-612.
17 Herodotus 2.112-20; see Pomeroy, pp.17-18.
18 *Suda* iv 323; Strabo 10.2.9.
19 Athenaeus 10.450e; 11.487a; 8.399c; 13.572c.
20 Porphyrion on Horace, *Epistles* 1.19.28. *Suda* iv 322s; P. Oxy 1800 fr. 1.
21 Ovid, *Heroides* 15.20.
22 Wilamowitz, p.56ff; Maximus of Tyre 18.9.
23 Bowra, pp.178, 238.
24 Lesky, p.146; Page, pp.143-4; Devereux, p.22.

25 Wilamowitz, p.56ff; Page, p.28ff.

26 Devereux, p.22.

27 See Tsagarakis, pp.69-82, for a detailed discussion of Sappho's use of the first person.

28 Hesiod, frag. 275, relates a myth in which Tiresias, who had been both male and female, is asked to solve a dispute between Zeus and Hera, the king and queen of the gods, about who enjoyed sex more, men or women. Tiresias replied that women enjoyed it nine times more than men. See also Murray, p.204.

29 Tiresias was also said to have been struck blind because he saw the goddess Athena bathing. See also the story of Gyges and Candaules, Herodotus 1.8-12.

30 See Pomeroy, p.47.

31 See Murray, pp.204-8.

32 Murray, pp.149, 204.

33 Anacreon 358*PMG*.

34 In Greek vase painting, 'courtship' was depicted by chin-chucking, the wearing or carrying of garlands and the exchange of gifts.

35 *Inscriptiones Graecae II² 10954*, see Lefkowitz and Fant, No.25.

36 Plato, *Symposium* 191e.

37 See McEvilley for a full discussion of imagination and memory in this fragment.

38 Dover, p.182.

39 See Murray, p.149.

40 See Marry.

41 See Dover, p.177.

42 Davison, p.226; Page, pp.95, 30, 83, 91ff.

43 Burn, p.229.

44 Praxilla: Zenobius 4.21; Corinna: Pausanias 9.22.3.

45 Corinna 664a*PMG*.

46 See Bowra, p.195.

47 See Campbell, *The Golden Lyre*, p.16; Page, pp.93-96.

48 Page, p.94.

49 Jenkyns, p.68.

50 See Page, p.90, note on *l*.8; Jenkyns, p.68; Campbell, *Greek Lyric Poetry*, p.280, note on *l*.8.

51 Philostratus Ep.51.

52 See Campbell, *The Golden Lyre*, p.17.

53 Page, pp.133, 110, 56.

54 Lesky, pp.142, 140.

55 Jenkyns, p.72.

56 See duBois for a full discussion of this fragment.

57 Hesiod, *Works and Days* 695-705.

58 See Arthur, p.72.

59 Alcaeus 42*LP*.

60 *Iliad* 24.762-75; 6.344-48; 3.173-76.

61 duBois, p.89.

62 *Palatine Anthology* 7.407: Dioscorides on Sappho.

SAPPHO AND TRANSLATION

Transcribing the poetry of one language into another is always a difficult task. For poetry is a distortion of language, the stretching of vocabulary, syntax and rhythm until they form new shapes – the creation of a language within a language now twice rather than once removed from the translator's reach. But as well as the difficulties faced by any translator of every poet – metre, word order and critical interpretation, amongst others – the translator of Sappho's poetry has first to deal with some fairly basic technical problems.

Although over two hundred fragments of her work have survived, some seven hundred lines in all, this represents a mere fraction of her complete output which probably amounted to five hundred poems. This severely limits the nature of any linguistic or critical analysis that can be made about her work, analysis which might in more normal circumstances provide the translator with important clues for their craft – the possible shading, for example, of a morally ambiguous term.

Secondly, the very process of that survival has caused several difficulties. Until the end of the nineteenth century, Sappho's poetry was known almost entirely from quotations in other classical writers, mainly anthologists, grammarians and literary commentators, for the most part writing a couple of centuries or more after Christ – nearly a millenium away from Sappho's original compositions. These quotations vary in length from a complete poem to a single word and their most common intention, to prove a point about dialect or metre, often has little to contribute to our understanding of their original context or literary skill.

In more modern times, a significant body of Sappho's work has been found on papyrus fragments, most of these in the sands of Oxyrhynchus, to the west of the Nile. But these too present their problems. Damage or wear to the papyri mean that the reading of certain words or phrases is ambiguous and a great deal of scholarship is devoted to ascertaining exactly what Sappho might have written. And while several contain almost complete poems, many more are far less rewarding. The last known use of the papyri, torn into strips for wrapping around mummified bodies, means that a great deal of Sappho's poetry reads only as follows in (a) below (88*LP*):

a)	b)
...you would wish...	...it must...
...little...	...to tell...
...be carried...	...loved yo...
...you know too...	...feeling...
...has forgotten...	...to think...
...someone might say...	...last time...
...I shall love...	...morning...
...as long as there is...	...the door...
...concerned...	...near me...
...a firm friend...	...you never...
...painful...	...again...
...bitter...	...let me...

Compare this to the second passage and the difficulties intensify; for where (a) represents the remnants of a poem considered worth preserving in antiquity in one of the great libraries of the east, whatever its later fate, (b) is a tattered piece of Basildon Bond retrieved from the rubbish blowing around a modern city street. The problem for scholar, literary historian and translator alike is how can we, or even how should we, convey the difference?

In the past, one solution has been to work around the fragments, filling in the gaps in order to make a more complete poem for the reader. The danger here is that over a large body of work in which most of the fragments are in the state above or even worse, a false voice emerges which has little to do with Sappho and much with the translator's own preconceptions or literary aspirations. Fortunately, the tendency in more recent years has been to present only what the original text supplies, unless the sense is quite clear and/or a sufficient body of scholarly opinion is agreed on its interpretation. Throughout these translations, I have followed this practice, indicating any conjectures with square brackets. Similarly, breaks at the start, end or during fragments of papyri are denoted by the use of dots. This also serves to distinguish between fragments that are found on papyrus, and those that are derived from quotations in ancient commentators, for the latter all commence with capitals.

Even where a substantial piece of text exists, with a relatively undisputed reading, as for example, No.78 (1*LP*), thought to be the only complete poem to survive or No.20 (31*LP*), the translator's path is still strewn with obstacles. Ancient commentators praised the smoothness of Sappho's style, the 'euphony' of her language, the choice and juxtaposition of her words. Unfortunately, this quality is one of the most difficult to capture in the transition from Greek to English; Greek has a far more flexible word order, a greater ability to mark emphasis, to use assonance or alliteration or to suggest ambiguity. In antiquity Sappho was also known for her skilful and innovative use of metre. Again this is extremely difficult, if not impossible, to render into English, as metre in Greek poetry is measured in length, in English by stress.

As in all Greek poetry, the oral origin of Sappho's work can also create a sense of distance for the modern reader. The poets of the *Iliad* and the *Odyssey*, often composing as they sung, used a string of stock epithets such as 'the wine dark sea' or 'rosy-fingered dawn' almost as mnemonics for their audience and themselves. A century or so later, Sappho and her lyric contemporaries, although working in a new and revolutionary genre, were still bound by the conventions and limitations of oral performance, if not composition. It is therefore not unusual for Sappho to repeat the same few adjectives throughout a poem, often within a few lines of each other, in a manner which might well seem unimaginative and dull to those of us more used to the luxury of the written word with all its opportunities for a second, third or fourth reading. It should also be noted that the Greek lexicon is far less extensive than English with the result that its vocabulary is far more flexible, allowing the same adjective to work in several different contexts with several shades of meaning. This is particularly the case in colour terminology; the Greek word *chloros*, for example, can mean anything from dark green to pale yellow (see note on No.20 [31*LP*]).

The difficulty for the translator is whether to recreate the repetitive sound and intention of the original Greek by reiterating the same word in English or to convey the ambiguity of Greek expression by substituting alternatives at each recurrence. In practice, the decision tends to be a case of considering each instance on its individual merits. For example, in No.78 (1*LP*), the repetition of the adverb *aute* 'again' is clearly a deliberate intention of style (see Page, pp.12-14), as Sappho mocks herself in her portrayal of Aphrodite's playfully exasperated response to yet another call for help in the poet's conquest of a loved one. In the fourth and fifth stanzas of No.74 (98*LP*), Sappho repeats the adjective *poikilos* to describe the headband she would like to obtain for her daughter. This instance is slightly complicated by the fact that the papyrus is damaged and a large block of text probably originally existed between the two stanzas. However, although *poikilos* could be translated in several different ways, such as 'many-coloured', 'spotted', 'embroidered' or 'finely-wrought' (although the latter more usually in the context of metalwork), I decided to repeat the phrase 'brightly-coloured' in order to contrast more strongly the specific headband which Sappho wishes for her daughter in the present with the purple band mentioned in the second stanza – an abstraction of the past and bound up with Sappho's memory of her mother.

Given such ambiguities, the preconceptions of those who attempt to interpret them come more and more into play. The most prevalent of these, which focus on Sappho's position as a woman, and their effect on readings of her work have already been discussed in the introduction above. Needless to say such assessments have had even more influence on the way in which her poems have been translated. For example, those who are worried by the eroticism of Sappho's poetry and seek to argue for a more spiritual tenure to her language have translated the Greek word *stromne* in the last stanza of No.32 (94*LP*) as anything from a 'mat' to a 'couch' whereas the term specifically refers to a bed – the place where you would spend the night. In the same stanza, the noun *pothos* has been translated as 'all that they wished for' or 'longing'. While technically correct (the term embraces any feeling of want for something absent), here as elsewhere in her poetry Sappho uses the word in the specific sense of sexual desire, particularly in conjunction with the verb *exienai*, 'to come to the end of', a phrase which, as Denys Page has pointed out, echoes an Homeric expression for sexual fulfilment (Page, p.79). At the opposite end of the spectrum, other translators have added their own speculations to the incomplete text of this stanza in order to provide a rather more titillating version of Sappho's eroticism: 'gently your desire/for delicate young women was satisfied', reads one, for example (Barnstone, p.71), echoing the lurid fantasies of Baudelaire, Verlaine and the other *fin de siècle* poets.

There is also a tendency for translators to trivialise the power of Sappho's writing by using a rather florid language perhaps thought appropriate for the work of a woman poet. For instance, the Greek adjective *agapetos* which describes an object of affection, something or someone that is worthy of love, is often translated as the rather trite 'darling' or 'my darling'. Again, in the last section of No.31 (58*LP*), the noun *habrosune* has been translated by 'delicacy' or 'refinement'. The Greek is problematic for it can mean 'material splendour' or even 'luxuriousness', as well as referring to the freshness of youth, with the sense of 'charm' or 'delicateness' more usually reserved for descriptions of literary style. In my translation, I have opted for 'intensity' because this seems to convey the meaning of vigour, as well as the riches of existence which the speaker is loath to leave behind, with none of the moral censure that 'luxuriousness' or 'sensuality' might convey.

The aim of my translations throughout has been to reproduce Sappho's poetry as faithfully as possible through a careful study of both text and critical readings, with the intention of avoiding, if the sense will allow, the twin pitfalls of addition and preconception. As for form, with the longer fragments and particularly with those poems that are almost complete, I have attempted, wherever possible, to retain the essence of Sappho's original. My aim here has been to ensure that the English text on the page approximates as directly as is practical, syllable for syllable, to that of the Greek. The brief fragments, however, are not so straightforward. A string of half-lines (as in No.29 [26*LP*]), a single word (No.55 [185*LP*]) or a second-hand description of a point of style (No.27 [197*LP*]) would be of little interest or use to the modern reader. Here in order to convey a sense of torn papyri or truncated quotation without losing any of their impact, I have taken the liberty of using freer, more modern forms of layout. These, I believe, are not only arresting to the reader but capture the essence of a splintered conversation or incomplete declaration of love, the intensity of an isolated metaphor. I have also tried to capture, without embellishment, the sensuality of Sappho's poetry, the clarity and strength of her style, the ease of her expression and the logical progression of her thought. In short, by preserving the form, content and tone of the original Greek, I have attempted to allow Sappho to speak for herself.

THE NEW FRAGMENTS:
Texts, Translations and Retranslations

'It is not very likely,' declared Bernard Grenfell and Arthur Hunt after their extraordinary discoveries during their first dig at Oxyrhynchus in 1896, 'that we shall find another poem of Sappho.'[1] Grenfell and Hunt's subsequent excavations in fact uncovered many other new fragments of the poet but even they might have been astonished to know that, over a hundred years later, new pieces of her work are still coming to light.

The first of these recent discoveries, contained on two papyri found in the collection of the University of Cologne in 2004 (and published by Martin West a year later), was technically not a new poem at all. Instead, here was a larger, more complete version of No. 31 (58*LP*), previously known from a tattered fragment unearthed in Oxyrhynchus and now housed in the collection of the Sackler Library Oxford.[2] In 2014, a perhaps even more remarkable development was announced by Dirk Obbink, head of the Oxyrhynchus Papyri Project at the University of Oxford; new pieces of privately-owned papyrus, given to Obbink for analysis, offered a staggering nine new readable texts of Sappho – the largest find since Grenfell and Hunt's excavations at Oxyrhynchus – with three containing previously unknown songs.[3] In addition, it seemed that all of these fragments came from the second half of Book 1 of the Alexandrian editions of Sappho. These, it was now clear, were collected by alphabetisation, confirming Hunt's theory on the ordering of her works by later editors.[4]

The Brothers Poem

Of all the new finds, most excitement centred on the so-called 'Brothers Poem' (No.121). This contains five complete Sapphic stanzas which are thought to represent most of the poem (an additional opening stanza is now believed to have been lost).[5] In the poem the poet reproaches an unnamed addressee for anticipating the safe return home of one Charaxus, presumably a merchant as he is expected 'ship laden' – a circumstance which, the speaker warns, should more properly be placed in the hands of the gods. The poem ends with the wish that another presumably younger, character Larichus, might revive the fortunes of both the speaker and her addressee.

Scholarly interest – and also some initial scepticism[6] – was raised by the characters' names: Charaxus and Larichus are both known from later sources as the apparent names of Sappho's elder and younger brothers. The fifth century B.C. Greek historian Herodotus, recounts that Charaxus bought and then freed the courtesan Rhodopis on a trip to Naucratis in Egypt, returning with her to Mytilene, much to the horror of Sappho who, Herodotus tells us, later vilified her brother in her songs (see note on No.81).[7] Other sources, such as Athenaeus, add that Charaxus was a trader or merchant, which again seems to fit with the Brothers Poem, while Strabo comments that Sappho called Rhopodis 'Doricha' in her poetry, a name which appears in No.81 (15*LP*) and possibly also in the very damaged fragment 7*LP*.[8]

Clearly the new fragment could be seen as representing a further piece of this story – Sappho's own. But as ever with ancient lyric poetry, caution is advised. Later sources often extrapolated a poet's biography back from their verse and, as discussed above in 'Sappho and Poetry', in a society in which choral lyrics represented an entire social group, the poet's 'I' can be problematic. Certainly discussions of the poem have been divided, with some scholars believing the addressee to be Sappho's mother. Others opt for her uncle, her brother Larichus, a third brother Eurygius or Rhodopis/ Doricha herself,[9] while a few dispute that the poem is about Sappho's brothers at all, arguing that they might be fictional characters.[10]

It might be more useful to consider the place of the fragment in Sappho's poetry as a whole. Like No. 21 (16*LP*), the Brothers Poem appears to rewrite Homeric epic; for instance, its three main protagonists – the speaker/Sappho, Charaxus and Larichus – could be seen to echo Penelope, Odysseus and Telemachus in the

Odyssey.[11] Other commentators note Sappho's use of Homeric language, for instance the rare Greek adjective *artemes* or 'safe' which occurs in the Odyssey of Odysseus's wish to return home from his voyage but also in the Iliad of the Trojan heroes Aeneas and Hector, as they return unharmed from battle.[12] As in Nos. 20 (31*LP*) and 78 (1*LP*), Sappho appears to be transposing male epic diction to the context of a female lyrical world in which the more usually silent Penelope becomes the voiced poet/narrator. On the other hand, the wily hero Odysseus – and even the epic warriors of Troy – are transformed into the absent, unvoiced Charaxus.[13] In translating such new pieces, it seemed important to apply the same approaches I had employed with the older Sappho fragments thirty-five years ago. For instance, for *artemes*, I settled on 'unscathed' to echo its use in both the *Iliad* and the *Odyssey*. In addition, I slightly elongated the description of the 'harsh storms' to summon up the many gales that Odysseus faces on his own travels.

There were other issues too. As Obbink has noted of the new poems, 'as many as four separate papyrus manuscripts contributed to the textual reconstruction of a single line'. He points to the fact that overlaps with existing papyrus fragments helped in this process yet could also produce 'frustratingly different readings'. Suggestions from other textual scholars also proved both help and hindrance, with these varying readings ranked 'in descending order of persuasiveness' in Obbink's critical apparatus.[14] Obbink has not been immune to such fluctuations himself, changing his mind on his own readings of the texts, often significantly, from his first 2014 publication to that of 2016.

The Cypris Song

Another poem found on the same piece of papyrus as the Brothers Poem, which Obbink calls the Kypris or Cypris Song (here No.122), has proved even more problematic. The poem addresses Cypris or Aphrodite, the goddess of love and desire, also invoked by Sappho in several other fragments (see Section VI).[15] The poem's complex opening questions to the goddess about the nature of desire echo those of Nos.21 (16*LP*) and 78 (1*LP*), while the central images of its more fragmentary second stanza – a desire which shakes the body and loosens the limbs – can also be found in Nos.1 (47*LP*) and 2 (130*LP*). Interestingly, the new text overlaps with another previously known, if mostly very damaged, fragment, part of which I had previously translated in No.29 (26*LP*). With more of the text, some of its then conjectured readings can be challenged. Placed in its proper context of a ritual or devotional song, it becomes an entirely new poem.[16]

One of the main difficulties with the Cypris Song is the number of different readings of the piece, particularly its tricky opening interrogative line. As Diane Rayor comments 'the foundation for reliable published translations is accurate Greek texts'.[17] Rayor had already had to stop the press for her new volume of Sappho for Cambridge University Press in 2014 when the new fragments came to light. She then worked her way through three versions as Obbink's text shifted and changed in the light of new readings and re-readings.[18] For my own translation (No.122), I have followed Obbink's latest 2016 text for its first stanza. However, at times I was reminded of translating Erinna's *Distaff* for my 1996 volume *Classical Women Poets* when I ended up with an enormous piece of paper with each scholar's emendations shaded in a different colour.[19]

The Green Collection Fragments

Another new series of papyri, acquired by the private Green Collection in Oklahoma City, was published by Obbink in 2014. Believed to be from the same papyrus roll as the Brothers Poem and the Cypris (or Kypris) Song, these have also proved extremely fruitful – and challenging.[20] One of the longer pieces is a new, more complete text of the extremely damaged fragment 9*LP*, which previously consisted of seven lines with about ten or so half-words in all. The new fragment is still quite damaged but now runs to twenty half-lines, with two mostly readable Sapphic stanzas. It now appears clear that the poet urges an addressee, 'mother', to make preparations for a religious festival (No.123).[21] This is presumably that of Hera who, with Zeus and Dionysus, was worshipped at the Sanctuary of the Three Gods at Messon on Lesbos, and in whose honour women's beauty contests were held there (she is also mentioned in the Brothers Poem, as well as in No.91 (17LP), on which see below, and No.127).[22] For its translation, I have followed Obbink's conjectures and, in its final lines, added a couple of my own, all marked by the use of square brackets, as in previous translations.

Another fragment in the group, fragment 16a (No.124), is also problematic. It may be the opening stanzas of a new poem that followed No. 21 (16LP), the Ode to Anactoria, in textual editions. Alternatively, in his latest textual edition of the new fragments, Obbink has argued that they might constitute a continuation of No.21 which many editors had previously thought complete.[23] The opening stanza appears to chime with the theme and concerns of much of Sappho's love poetry; the nature of desire and the ways in which the lover might find happiness. As Obbink has noted, it also features a typically Sapphic progression from generalised experience ('No, it is not possible for anyone/to be completely happy...') to that of the individual, whether or not identified as the poet herself.[24]

Its second stanza is far more incomplete but nevertheless contains some startling images. In line 6 of the fragment the words *ep'akras*, or literally 'on the edges', could refer to a Greek expression for 'on tiptoes'.[25] The following line appears to have an equally arresting reference to *chion*, in Homer used of fallen snow. This could evoke the figure of Kairos or 'Opportunity', the concept of acting at the correct time or seizing the day, which in Greek art and mythology was often portrayed as a young man running on tiptoes. But *ep'akras* was also used of being 'on the edge' of a changing season, particularly spring, which chimed with the later mention of (perhaps melting) snow. In addition, the verb which Obbink reads as *ebas*, or 'you went' echoes the *eba* ('she went') used of Helen's desertion of Paris in No.21 (16LP).[26] And so I added in some conjectures here to include the image of a lover leaving like fleeting snow in the spring.

Another, tiny fragment, No.126 (fragment 18a), is thought to be part of a previously unknown poem, although its reference to the night and stars (and possibly also an exhortation to drink), brings to mind Nos. 27 (197*LP*) and 111 (34*LP*). My approach to the translation of such tiny pieces here has been the same as that of my original edition, using free modernist poetic forms to represent a hanging, isolated image, frozen in time by its circumstance of survival (see 'Sappho and Translation' above).[27]

As well as fleshing out previously very corrupted texts, the new papyri also provide new insights into longer fragments, quite literally filling in some gaps in their lines. For instance, one piece offers two more words for the missing lines of the third stanza of No.21 (16*LP*), just as the poem turns from the example of the mythological Helen back to the passion of Sappho herself. Intriguingly, both of these words, 'mind' and 'thinks' (*voemma* and *voesei*), refer to cognition but stretching out the meaning any further is still a matter of conjecture.[28]

The missing opening word of No.80 (5*LP*) was assumed to be the goddess Aphrodite, addressed again as 'Cypris', alongside the Nereids or sea-nymphs of its first line. The new papyrus reveals the word to be instead a qualifying adjective for the nymphs, *potniai* or 'revered'. Yet, true to form, there is already a scholarly debate over its reading, with some arguing that the word might be *pontiai* or 'sea-dwelling', an epithet often employed of ocean deities.[29]

In No.91 (17*LP*), the changes were even more radical. Previous texts of the fragment offered only the left hand side of the poem whereas the new papyrus has the left and right sides for most of its twenty lines, with only some central words missing, making it possible 'to follow a narrative we could only guess at before'.[30] And so, the previously conjectured opening invocation of Hera is now known to have been instead a call to celebrants to partake in her festival (see above). Such small but significant changes continue throughout the new text so I have now produced a new revised version of the fragment (No.127).

Retranslation and the Cologne Fragment

To general readers, it might seem disquieting that any translation of an ancient text is not definitive; that what they read in a published volume might not be static, monolithic, fixed. For a translator, too, it is sometimes difficult to have to accept that, having taken hours and hours of research and reading, of poring over a difficult and already disputed text, not to mention agonising over semantic choices in the target language, a translation might no longer be valid or, worst of all, no longer correct. Yet there can be pleasures in this sinuous, ever-flowing art. More than ever, translation becomes part of the dialogue. Translation moves the text forwards. As I wrote in my 2013 study *Piecing Together The Fragments*, 'it is through translation that ancient fragments can revive their dead, silent language...translation can go further into scholarship's uncharted regions, unperturbed by the unknown'.[31]

When it came to retranslating No.31 (58*LP*), the Tithonus poem, after the discovery of a new, almost complete text in Cologne, such statements proved prophetic. Previously, when working on the much more incomplete poem, I had felt a strong affinity to the fragment, so much so that it became the one exception to my rule of not filling in the gaps (although I added a page note to that effect). The poem's reconstruction was greatly aided by its reference to the myth of Tithonus and Eös, the immortal Dawn, who gave her lover eternal life but neglected to offer him eternal youth until he was so shrivelled with age that he was transformed into the cicada. So, when West's new, more complete, text appeared in 2005, it was very gratifying to discover that my conjectures followed this new poem quite closely. If translation is an activity that occupies the realms of inspiration and creativity, as well as the pages of the dictionary, then it was also cheering to find that it embraced serendipity as well.

Nevertheless, when I was asked to provide a version of West's new text for Poet in the City's 'Sappho...Fragments' event at the Bloomsbury Theatre, London in October 2013, the two texts had become so entwined in my mind that they proved harder to disentangle than I could have imagined. In the end, to distinguish a new version from my earlier reconstruction, I decided to use more formal, less conversational semantics in English than previously. Yet I still found it difficult to keep to the six couplets of West's reconstruction without writing prose lines so the text was transmuted into an almost-sonnet of fourteen lines. Nevertheless, thirty years – and two millennia later – it still felt as if Sappho was at my shoulder as I wrote.

Such challenges underline the difficulty of producing any definitive version of these fluid and always shifting texts. The next few years might well see more fragments coming to light which will negate the translations here, both new and old. But this is not only to be expected but welcomed. Each new version marks a new staging point in an ancient text's long, long history. Each one represents Pound's 'blood brought to ghosts', each performs an act of poetic necromancy, conjuring up fresh, breathing poems.[32] 'Good luck in the gravedigging,' Bernard Grenfell's brother had scribbled on a postcard to the archaeologist before he left for Oxyrhynchus. Fortunately for all of us those graves are still offering up their secrets.

Notes

1. Grenfell & Hunt, p. vi.
2. P. Oxy. 1787.
3. A full discussion of their texts can be found in Burris, Fish & Obbink; Obbink 2014, 2015, 2016a and 2016b.
4. See Obbink 2016b, p.41.
5. See Obbink 2016a, pp.25-26.
6. For instance, before publishing the text and translation of the Brothers Poems in the *TLS*, Mary Beard wrote to Martin West for an opinion on the poem's quality and authenticity. He replied: 'My initial impression was that it was very poor stuff, and linguistically problematic. But the more I looked at it the more Ok it seems. It's certainly not her best but it has her DNA all over it.' Quoted in Obbink 2016b, p.53.
7. Herodotus, 2, 135.
8. Athenaeus, 13, 596cd; Strabo,17.1.33.

9. See Obbink 2016c; Stehle; Lardinois; Bowie.
10. See also Lidov who notes that the brother mentioned in No.80 (5LP) is not named as Charaxus while Charaxus in the Brothers Poem is not explicitly revealed to be Sappho's brother.
11. See Kurke; Mueller.
12. *Odyssey* 13.43. See Bär. *Iliad*, 5.515; 7.308.
13. By contrast Ewen Bowie believes this and other songs were performed at male symposiums.
14. Obbink 2016a, 14 ff.
15. See Obbink 2014; 2016a, pp.26-27.
16 P. Oxy 1231 fr.16. These lines are also echoed in No. 124.
17 Rayor, 2016, p.400.
18. Ibid.p.396 ff. As well as Obbink's own revisions, M.L. West also produced a significantly different text – and translation – of the poem's first stanza.
19. See Balmer 1996; 2013 pp.116-117.
20. See Burris, Fish & Obbink; Obbink 2016a, pp.17-25.
21. P. Oxy. 2289 fr.4. Sappho also mentions a (her?) mother in Nos. 40 (102*LP*), 74 (98*LP*) and 110 (104a*LP*).
22. Although a half-word in the old fragment usually read as 'Hera' is here shown instead to read '*ωραι*' or 'the seasons' (particularly springtime).
23. See, for example, Campbell, 1982, p.67.
24. Obbink 2016b pp.48-49.
25. Obbink 2016a p.29.
26. On the use of *eba* in Greek women's poetry, see Balmer 1996 p.17; 29; 60. 2013 p.119; 125.
27. A longer discussion can also be found in Balmer 2013 pp.92-96.
28. Obbink suggests 'for she [Cypris?] with unbending mind/accomplishes easily whatever she thinks' (2016a p.29).
29. See, for example, West 2014 p.5 who points out that Pindar uses the epithet of the Nereids in *Pythian Odes*, 11.2.
30. Rayor 2016 p.408.
31. Balmer 2013 p.231.
32. See Kenner, 1971 p.150.
33. Now in the Ashmolean Collection. An image can be found at http://www.papyrology.ox.ac.uk/POxy/VExhibition/images/postcard.jpg

Key to the Translations

[ ]   denotes a conjectural meaning
. . .   denotes a break in the papyrus
***** denotes the end of a fragment

The text used is *Poetarum Lesbiorum Fragmenta,* ed. Edgar Lobel et Denys Page (Oxford 1955, repr. 1963).

The text used for the new fragments is that of Dirk Obbink in 'The Newest Sappho: Text, Apparatus Criticus, and Translation' from Anton Bierl and André Lardinois (eds.), *The Newest Sappho: P. Sapph. Obbink and P. GC inv. 105, frs.1-4.* (Leiden: Brill, 2016), 13-33.

I.

LOVE

1

Love shook my heart
like the wind on the mountain
rushing over the oak trees[†]

*****

2

Love makes me tremble yet again
sapping all the strength from my limbs;

bittersweet, undefeated creature –
against you there is no defence[‡]

*****

3

Stand up and look at me face to face,
friend to friend;
unfurl the loveliness in your eyes

*****

[††] See also No.122.

4

On a soft cushion

> I will soothe my tired body

*****

5

[I ran after you]
like a small child

> flying

>> to her mother

*****

6

I tell you;

> in time to come,
someone will remember us

*****

7

[From our love]
I want neither
the sweetness of honey

              nor the sting of the bees

*****

8

I do not expect
          to touch the sky

*****

9

[My advice to you is:]
don't disturb
        the jetsam
           [on the beach]

*****

10

I do not have a spiteful temper
                              but a tender heart

                    *****

11

                    Beautiful women,
my feelings for you
will never falter

                    *****

12

May you sleep on the breast
                    of your tender companion

                    *****

13

Night crept up on them

                        black sleep closed their eyes

*****

14

. . . for whenever I look at you,
it seems to me that not even
Hermione is your equal;
no, far better to compare you
to Helen, whose hair was golden . . .

*****

15

I do not believe

                        the light of day will ever see
another woman,

                        now, or in time to come, who will
rival you in skill

*****

16

. . . bind together, Dicca, with your slender hands, shoots of dill,
wreathe garlands around your lovely hair;
for the Graces favour a woman crowned with blossom
but turn away from those who go ungarlanded . . .

*****

17

Mnasidica,
   more lovely even
      than slender Gyrinno

*****

18

  . . . Atthis,
    for you . . .

*****

19

. . . for you, I will leave behind

[all that I love . . .]

*****

II.

DESIRE

20

It seems to me that man is equal to the gods,
that is, whoever sits opposite you
and, drawing nearer, savours, as you speak,
the sweetness of your voice

and the thrill of your laugh, which have so stirred the heart
in my own breast, that whenever I catch
sight of you, even if for a moment,
then my voice deserts me

and my tongue is struck silent, a delicate fire
suddenly races underneath my skin,
my eyes see nothing, my ears whistle like
the whirling of a top

and sweat pours down me and a trembling creeps over
my whole body, I am greener than grass;[†]
at such times, I seem to be no more than
a step away from death;

but all can be endured since even a pauper . . .

*****

[†]*greener than grass:* this phrase has caused many scholars a great deal of
difficulty. It is often translated as 'paler than grass' and thought to refer to
the colour draining from the speaker's face. Greek colour terms are far
vaguer than those in English; the adjective *chloros* could mean both brilliant
green and pale yellow. However, it was used to describe the rich colour of
foliage and, as Lefkowitz has argued, may well be an echo of the Homeric
phrase 'green fear' which refers to the warrior's fear in battle.

21[†]

Some an army on horseback, some an army on foot
and some say a fleet of ships is the loveliest sight
on this dark earth; but I say it is what-
ever you desire:

and it is perfectly possible to make this clear
to all; for Helen, the woman who by far surpassed
all others in her beauty, left her husband –
the best of all men –

behind and sailed far away to Troy; she did not spare
a single thought for her child nor for her dear parents
but [the goddess of love] led her astray
[to desire . . .]

                    [. . . which][‡]
reminds me now of Anactoria
although far away,

whose long-desired footstep, whose radiant, sparkling face
I would rather see before me than the chariots
of Lydia or the armour of men
who fight wars on foot . . .

                    ****

---

† See also No.124 which may be a continuation of this poem.
‡ For a discussion of a new papyrus find, which might add a few words to
this stanza, see 'The New Fragments: Texts, Translations and Retranslations'.

22†

[. . . come here tonight,] I beg, you, Gongyla,
take up your lyre [and sing to us;]
for once again an aura of desire
hovers around

your beauty, your dress thrills all those who see you
and the heart in my breast quickens;
once I too poured scorn on Aphrodite,
goddess of love,

but now I pray [that you will soon be here . . .]
oh, I wish [we were never parted . . .]

*****

†This poem is very fragmentary and the text is corrupt.

23

[Her voice was]
>far sweeter than any flute . . .

[her hair,]
>more golden than gold . . .

[and her skin,]
>far whiter than an egg . . .

*****

24

And wrapped around her . . .
>a soft linen robe

*****

25

>And on her feet

bright coloured sandals,
skilful Lydian work . . .

*****

26

You've come and you –

        oh, I was longing for you –

have cooled my heart

        which was burning with desire

*****

27

[I want you to know;]
I prayed that for us

        the night

            could last twice as long

*****

28

[I was dreaming of you but]
just then
Dawn, in her golden sandals

        [woke me]

*****

III.

DESPAIR

29[†]

. . . I know it is true;

        those that I love best
        do me the most harm . . .

*****

30

[I tell you I am miserable,]
Gongyla . . .
in fact an omen . . .

[I dreamt that Hermes] appeared before me:
'Lord,' I told him, 'I swear by the blessed goddess[‡]
that I can find no pleasure here on earth
but I am possessed by a strange longing to die,
to see the river at the gates of hell,
whose banks are overgrown with lotus, wet with dew,
the Acheron . . .'

*****

[†] See also No.122
[‡] *the blessed goddess:* Aphrodite.

31[†]

. . . already old age is wrinkling my
skin and my hair is turning from black
to grey; my knees begin to tremble
and my legs no longer carry me . . .
oh but once, once we were like young deer
. . . what can I do? . . .

         . . . it is not possible
to return to my youth; for even
Eös,[‡] the dawn – whose arms are roses,
who brings light to the ends of the earth –
found that old age embraced Tithonus,[‡]
her immortal lover . . .

         . . . I know I must die . . .
yet I love the intensity of life
and this and desire keep me here in
the brightness and beauty of the sun
[and not with Hades . . .]

*****

[†]The text of the poem is very fragmentary and much of this translation is conjectural. For a translation of the recently-discovered, more complete text of this fragment, see No.128.

[‡]*Eös, Tithonus:* Eös, the dawn goddess, fell in love with Tithonus, a mortal. She asked Zeus to give him immortality but forgot to ask for eternal youth. Eventually he became old and shrivelled and talked endlessly. Eös looked after him and finally turned him into the cicada.

32

. . . frankly I wish that I were dead:
she was weeping as she took her leave from me

and many times she told me this:
'Oh what sadness we have suffered,
Sappho, for I'm leaving you against my will.'

So I gave this answer to her:
'Go, be happy but remember
me there, for you know how we have cherished you,

if not, then I would remind you
[of the joy we have known,] of all
the loveliness that we have shared together;

for many wreaths of violets,
of roses and of crocuses
. . . you wove around yourself by my side

. . . and many twisted garlands
which you had woven from the blooms
of flowers, you placed around your slender neck

. . . and you were anointed with
a perfume, scented with blossom,
. . . although it was fit for a queen

and on a bed, soft and tender
. . . you satisfied your desire . . .'

*****

33

[. . . Atthis,]
although she is in Sardis,
her thoughts often stray here, to us . . .

[. . . for you know that she honoured] you
as if you were a goddess
and, most of all, delighted in your song.

But now she surpasses all the women
of Lydia, like the moon,
rose-fingered, after the sun has set,

shining brighter than all the stars; its light
stretches out over the salt-
filled sea and the fields brimming with flowers:

the beautiful dew falls and the roses
and the delicate chervil
and many-flowered honey-clover bloom.

But wandering here and there, she recalls
gentle Atthis with desire
and her tender heart is heavy with grief . . .

*****

34

Atthis, you have come to hate the thought of me;
these days, you fly to Andromeda instead

*****

35

Once upon a time, I loved you, Atthis,

yes, long ago . . .
even when I thought of you as a girl

small and graceless . . .

*****

36

You have forgotten me;
oh, who in the world

do you love better than me?

*****

37

How could
some yokel cast a spell on your heart –
doesn't she wear some yokel costume
and have no idea how to lift
her rags above her ankles?

*****

38†

The moon has set
                    and the stars have faded,
midnight has gone,
                    long hours pass by, pass by;
I sleep alone

*****

†One of Sappho's most famous fragments, although many scholars argue against
her authorship.

39[†]

I want to tell you something but shame prevents me . . .

if you truly desired something honest or good
and your tongue were not concocting some new evil,
there would be no shame in your eyes
and you would plead your cause outright . . .

*****

40

Mother dear, I simply cannot weave my cloth;
                                   I'm overpowered
by desire for a slender youth – and it's all
                                   Aphrodite's fault

*****

[†]Aristotle claimed that this fragment was a dialogue between Sappho and her male contemporary, Alcaeus. The first line has been seen as part of Alcaeus's speech and the rest as Sappho's reply. There is no other evidence to support this claim and here, as in other translations, I have concentrated on the actual evidence of the text rather than later interpretations.

41

If you really love me,
choose a younger wife;

for I, being older,
could not bear to live
[with a younger man . . .]

*****

42

Andromeda has been repaid
                    in full

*****

43

Irana!
Never before have I found you so tiresome

*****

44

I have had quite enough
                    of Gorgo

*****

45

[Gorgo!]
Many greetings to the daughter
                    of so many kings[†]

*****

46

. . . Micca . . . I won't allow it . . .
you prefer the love of women
                    descended from Penthilus . . .[†]

*****

[†]*of so many kings:* the Greek is a pun on the family name, Polyanactidae, one of the rival aristocratic factions in Mytilene.

46

. . . Micca . . . I won't allow it . . .
you prefer the love of women

        descended from Penthilus . . .†

*****

47

[I cannot bear it;]
. . . Archeanassa

      is Gorgo's lover . . .

*****

48

I don't know what to do –

      I'm torn in two

*****

†*Penthilus:* a mythical hero from whom the Penthilidae, another of the rival family factions at Mytilene, claimed descent.

49

I desire and yearn
          [for you]

*****

50

Pain drips
          through me

*****

51

You burn me

*****

52

As long as you wish

*****

53

. . . remember . . .
. . . we did the same

        in our youth . . .

*****

54

[When I was young and in love,]

        I too wove garlands

*****

IV.

MARRIAGE

55

A honey-voiced woman

  [sang at the wedding]

*****

56

. . . take up your lyre;

  sing of the bride
  whose dress is violet . . .

*****

57

[. . . sing of] the bride

  whose feet are graceful . . .

*****

58

. . . we are going

        to a wedding . . .

*****

59

. . . all night long, [at your door,
bridegroom,] women sang of the love
between you and your bride whose dress
is the colour of violets;

but come now, wake up; go and fetch
the young men, your companions;
tonight we shall see no more sleep
than the clear-voiced nightingale

*****

60

Beautiful woman

        graceful bride

*****

61

'We give this woman away,'

her father said

*****

62

Lucky bridegroom,
the marriage you have prayed for has come to pass
and the bride you dreamed of is yours . . .

Beautiful bride,
to look at you gives joy; your eyes are like honey,
love flows over your gentle face . . .

Aphrodite
has honoured you above all others

*****

63

Bridegroom,
> no woman was ever lovelier
>> [than your bride]

*****

64

To what, my dear bridegroom, should I compare you best?
I should compare you best to a slender sapling

*****

65[†]

Raise up the rooftop
(shout hymen!)
higher, carpenters,
(shout hymen!)
here comes the bridegroom, Ares' equal
and taller than the tallest giant

*****

66

The door-keeper's feet are seven yards long
and his shoes were stitched from five ox-hides;
ten cobblers worked day and night to make them

*****

[†]*65 and 66* have often been cited by scholars as evidence of Sappho's
heavy-handed sense of humour and lack of subtlety. Yet they are important
evidence of Sappho's celebration of women's experience. The poems were
probably sung as the bridal procession moved from the bride's to the groom's
house, at the climax of the ceremony. The comparison of the groom in 65 to
Ares, the god of war, and the ridicule of his heroic stature satirises male values.
Again, in 66, the door-keeper was a friend of the groom who guarded the
groom's house against the ritual attempt of the bride's attendants to "rescue"
her.

67

Farewell, bride, farewell,

        farewell, honoured bridegroom

*****

68

VIRGINITY

    . . . like the sweet-apple
turning red at the top of the highest branch,
forgotten by the apple gatherers – no,
not quite forgotten, for they could not reach so far . . .

*

    . . . like the hyacinth
on the mountains which shepherds tread under foot,
staining the earth with its purple flower . . .

*****

69

[Why am I unhappy?]
Am I still longing

>   for my lost virginity?

*****

70

[I assure you:]
I will remain a virgin

>   for ever

*****

71

BRIDE: Virginity, virginity,

>   have you deserted me, where have you gone?

VIRGINITY: I will never return to you again,

>   never return to you again

*****

72

THE MARRIAGE OF HECTOR AND ANDROMACHE

A herald came . . . Idaeus . . . swift messenger . . .

'Hector and his companions are bringing a woman
with sparkling eyes, graceful Andromache, from sacred Thebe,
from the ever-flowing streams of Placia, in their ships
across the salt-filled sea;
          and with her they also carry
many golden bracelets, purple clothing, engraved trinkets,
ivory and silver goblets too numerous to count.'
This was Idaeus' speech.
          And Hector's beloved father[†]
nimbly leapt up and the word spread throughout the wide city
to those who held Hector dear.
          At once the sons of Ilus[‡]
yoked mules to broad-wheeled carts and a crowd of women and girls
whose ankles were slim, climbed on, while the daughters of Priam . . .

. . . and the sweet music of the flute was mingled with the clash
of castanets and the young women sang a sacred song
so clearly that their wondrous echo reached the sky . . .

. . . and in the streets, the mingled scents of myrrh and cassia
and frankincense;
          with one voice the elder women shouted
for joy and with a clear cry all the men called on Paean,[§]
the noble archer, the skilled lyre player and they all sang
in praise of Hector and Andromache who were like gods

[†]*beloved father:* Priam, king of Troy.
[‡]*Ilus:* founder of Troy.
[§]*Paean:* the god, Apollo.

A bowl of ambrosia
was mixed with water.

Hermes took up the pitcher,
served wine to the gods.

Then they all raised their goblets
and poured libations

and they offered the bridegroom
all kind of blessings

*****

V.

MOTHER AND DAUGHTER

74

. . . my mother [used to say that]
in her youth it was thought to be
very fine to bind up your hair

with a dark purple [headband] – yes,
extremely fine indeed, although
for a girl whose hair is golden

like a torch flame [better] to wreathe
in it garlands of fresh flowers;
recently [I saw] a headband,

brightly coloured, from Sardis . . .

but for you, Cleis,[†] I do not have
a brightly coloured headband nor
do I know where I may find one . . .

*****

75

I have a beautiful daughter, golden
like a flower, my beloved Cleis,
for her, in her place, I would not accept
the whole of Lydia, nor lovely . . .

*****

[†]*Cleis:* according to one ancient biography, the name of both Sappho's
mother and her daughter.

76

There is no place for grief, [Cleis,][†]
in a house which serves the Muse;
our own is no exception

*****

77

[I once saw]
a gentle little girl

        gathering flowers

*****

†*Cleis:* Maximus of Tyre, who quotes this fragment, records that it is
addressed to Sappho's daughter.

VI.

THE GODDESS
OF LOVE

78

Immortal Aphrodite, on your patterned throne,
daughter of Zeus, guile-weaver,
I beg you, goddess, don't subjugate my heart
with anguish, with grief

but come here to me now, if ever in the past
you have heard my distant pleas
and listened; leaving your father's golden house
you came to me then

with your chariot yoked; beautiful swift sparrows
brought you around the dark earth
with a whirl of wings, beating fast, from heaven
down through the mid-air

to reach me quickly; then you, my sacred goddess,
your immortal face smiling,
asked me what had gone wrong this time and this time
why was I begging

and what in my demented heart, I wanted most:
'Who shall I persuade this time
to take you back, yet once again, to her love;
who wrongs you, Sappho?

For if she runs away, soon she shall run after,
if she shuns gifts, she shall give,
if she does not love you, soon she shall even
against her own will.'

So come to me now, free me from this aching pain,
fulfil everything that
my heart desires to be fulfilled: you, yes you,
will be my ally.

*****

79[†]

Leave Crete and come to me now, to that holy temple,
where the loveliness of your apple grove
waits for you and your altars smoulder
with burning frankincense;

there, far away beyond the apple branches, cold streams
murmur, roses shade every corner
and, when the leaves rustle, you are seized
by a strange drowsiness;

there, a meadow, a pasture for horses, blooms with all
the flowers of Spring, while the breezes blow
so gently . . .

there . . . Cyprian goddess, take and pour
gracefully like wine into golden cups,
a nectar mingled with all the joy
of our festivities

*****

[†]*79:* The text of this fragment comes from a potsherd of the third century
B.C. Campbell (1982, p.57) points out that the poem does not necessarily
begin here as the participle 'coming down from' and part of a noun (heaven?
mountain?) precede it.

80

[Cypris and] Nereids,† grant that my brother‡
will return here to me without harm and that
everything which he wishes for in his heart
will come to pass;

grant that he atone for all his former crimes
and become a joy to his friends, a torment
to his enemies and let no one ever cause
us grief again;

grant too that he may wish his sister to have
her share of honour, and wretched sorrow . . .

*****

†*Cypris and Nereids:* Cypris: Aphrodite, invoked as goddess of the sea.
Nereids: sea-nymphs. A new papyrus find has shown that, rather than 'Cypris',
the poem's opening word is instead the adjective *potniai*, or 'revered', used of
the Nereids. See 'The New Fragments: Texts, Translations and Retranslations'.

‡*brother:* some ancient sources name Sappho's brother as Charaxus, a wine-
merchant. This fragment might well refer to the political troubles in Mytilene
during Sappho's lifetime and to her family's involvement in them. See also
No.122.

81

. . . may she find even you, Cypris, too severe
and, as for Doricha,[†] may she never boast
that she returned for a second time
to the love she had longed for

*****

82

[Aphrodite, come to me]
whether you are at Cyprus

        or Paphos

             or Panormus

*****

[†]*Doricha:* according to the historian, Herodotus, Charaxus, Sappho's
brother, fell in love with and freed a courtesan of Naucratis, called Rhodopis.
When he returned to Mytilene, Herodotus continued, his sister ridiculed him
in verse. Several centuries later, another ancient writer, Strabo, wrote that
Sappho called Rhodopis, Doricha, although yet another, Athenaeus, rejected
this. Modern scholars usually accept Strabo's comment and identify this frag-
ment as Sappho's poem against her brother. See also No.121 and 'The New
Fragments: Texts, Translations and Retranslations'.

83

Aphrodite,
your garlands are made of golden leaves;

if only I
could have a share in such good fortune

*****

84

[Goddess of love,]
to you I will sacrifice

a white goat

*****

85

Sappho,
why spurn Aphrodite

whose blessings are many?

*****

86

In a dream
I spoke with Aphrodite

                the Cyprian goddess

*****

87

[She said to me:]
'Sappho, you and my servant, Eros . . .'

*****

88[†]

[Eros came down from heaven,]
his dark purple cloak
wrapped around him . . .

*****

89[†]

[Eros, the god of desire,]
brings pain
            weaves tales
[for mortals . . .]

*****

90

Persuasion is
            Aphrodite's daughter;

it is she who beguiles
            our mortal hearts

*****

[†]*88 and 89:* the ancient sources which quote these fragments, Pollux and
Maximus of Tyre, comment that they are descriptions of Eros. See also
No.125.

VII.

RELIGION

Appear to me, lady Hera,[‡] I beg you,
reveal your graceful form; for it was you who
once answered the prayers of the Atridae,[§]
illustrious kings:

after many trials, both near Troy and at sea,
they came here, to Lesbos, but they could not leave,
could not complete their journey home until
they had summoned you

and Zeus, suppliants' god, and Dionysus,
Thyone's[*] lovely son; so be gracious now,
send your help to me now as you have helped
others in the past . . .

*****

[†] For a new version of this fragment, based on recent papyri finds, see No.127.

[‡] *Hera:* goddess who represents women, worshipped on Lesbos where, at her annual festival, female beauty was celebrated.

[§] *Atridae:* a reference to an incident in the Odyssey (3.130ff). The Atridae are the sons of Atreus, king of Mycenae – Menelaus, king of Sparta, husband of Helen; and Agamemnon, the commander-in-chief of the Greek forces at Troy. On their way home to Greece after the Trojan War, the brothers quarrelled; Menelaus thought it best to sail home immediately while Agamemnon stayed in Troy. Menelaus came to Lesbos where he prayed to Zeus for guidance. In Sappho's poem, Agamemnon does not argue with Menelaus but is present on Lesbos. The brothers do not pray only to Zeus but also to Hera and Dionysus, the other deities particularly worshipped on Lesbos.

[*] *Thyone:* a name given to Semele, Dionysus' mother and daughter of Cadmus of Thebes, after her deification.

92

When the full moon rose
women took their place
around the altar . . .

*****

93

[. . . they were dancing]
as Cretan women once danced
beside a lovely altar,
their graceful feet treading down
the smooth soft bloom of the grass

*****

94

Alas for Adonis

*****

95

Gentle Adonis is dying, Cytherea,[†]
what should we do?

Beat your breasts, young women, tear your tunics
[and mourn for him]

*****

96

They say that long ago
Leda[†] once found an egg;

it was the colour of
a hyacinth . . .

*****

[†]*Cytherea:* Aphrodite, so called because the island of Cythera in the Aegean was said to have been her birthplace.

[†]*Leda:* in Greek mythology, wife of Tyndareus, king of Sparta, and raped by Zeus in the form of a swan. She laid two eggs; from one were hatched the twins, Castor and Pollux, from the other, Helen of Troy.

Leto and Niobe[1] were

the very best of friends

*****

---

[1] *Leto and Niobe*: Leto: mother of the gods, Apollo and Artemis. Niobe: mother of seven daughters and seven sons, she boasted that she was therefore superior to Leto, although Leto's two children were divine. Apollo and Artemis then killed Niobe's children in revenge. Niobe wept for them continuously and became a column of stone from which her tears continued to flow.

VIII.

POETRY
AND THE
MUSES

98[†]

My dearest friends
today I will sing with a clear voice
            to enchant you all

* * * * *

99

Come, my lovely tortoise-shell lyre;
my music will give you speech

* * * * *

100[‡]

My words may only be of air
            but they will always give pleasure

* * * * *

†See also No. 125
‡This fragment is quoted by Edmonds and comes from a painting of Sappho on an Attic vase c.430 B.C.

101

The singer from Lesbos
surpasses all of those

from other lands

*****

102

Come here, to me, rose-like Graces;

Muses, [bind up] your lovely hair

*****

103

Arms like roses,

daughters of Zeus,
sacred Graces,

come to me here

*****

104

Come here to me, to me, Muses;

       leave your golden house

    *****

105

[It is the Muses]

    who have brought me honour
    through the gift of their art

    *****

106

[Sappho said:]

The Muses have made me happy
in my lifetime

and when I die
I shall never be forgotten[†]

    *****

[†]According to ancient commentators, Sappho was the first to say that poetry brings the poet immortality.

107[†]

When you die, you will lie unremembered for ever more;
for you there will be no regret, no share in the roses
of Pieria;[‡] invisible in Hades, as on earth,
you will wander aimlessly among the unknown dead . . .

*****

108

. . . but now my dear friends

> [let us end our song;]
> it is almost day[§] . . .

*****

[†]Stobaeus quoted this fragment and claimed that it was addressed to a woman
of no education. Plutarch also wrote that it was to a rich woman or an igno-
rant woman, without culture. Modern commentators cite it as an example of
Sappho's bitchiness. However, as the fragment stands, its tone is as much
elegiac as satirical.

[‡]*Pieria:* In Macedonia, birthplace of the Muses.

[§]*day:* Campbell (1982, p.87) argues that this line represents the end of the
poem, composed, he says, for some night time festival.

IX.

NATURE
AND
WISDOM

109

[The evening star –]
the most beautiful
                    of all the stars

                    *****

110

Hesperus, you bring everything that
                    the light-tinged dawn has scattered;

you bring the sheep, you bring the goat, you bring
                    the child back to its mother

                    *****

111

The stars around the lovely moon
hide their brightness when it is full
and shines the clearest over all
the earth

                    *****

112[†]

[The moon is]
        like silver

*****

113

Golden broom grew
        along the shore

*****

114

The nightingale is
        the harbinger of spring
        and her voice is desire

*****

[†]This fragment may well be part of a simile, like that in 33, which compares the beauty of a woman who surpasses her companions to the moon outshining the stars.

115[†]

[. . . like frightened doves]
whose hearts turn to ice

        whose wings falter . . .

*****

116

Death must be an evil – and the gods agree;
for why else would they live for ever?

*****

117

Gold is the child of the gods;
it will never decay
and cannot be corrupted

*****

---

†This fragment is quoted in a commentary on Pindar which says that it
comes from a description of doves.

118

[Sappho's advice was:]
when someone sows anger in your heart,
keep quiet;

      curb your thoughtless, barking tongue

*****

119

Beauty endures only for as long as it can be seen;
goodness, beautiful today, will remain so tomorrow

*****

120

Wealth without virtue is
               a harmful companion;
but a mixture of both,
        the happiest friendship

*****

X.

THE NEW FRAGMENTS

121

('BROTHERS POEM')[†]

You keep talking of Charaxus coming home,
his ship laden. But I believe these are things
only Zeus and his fellow gods can foretell.
You need not worry

but instead send for me and then call on me
to beseech Queen Hera over and over
that Charaxus might steer with care, a safe ship
to reach home at last

and find us both unscathed. Everything else
we have to entrust to the hands of the gods;
for after wild, blustering gales, fair weather
all at once blows in

and to those the King of Olympus[ι] decides
to send a helpmate, his own guiding spirit
to free them from their toil, happiness will come,
a wealth of blessings.

So for us. If Larichus, too, can now raise
his sights and become the man he truly could
then the many great weights dragging at our souls
will suddenly lift.

*****

[†] *Brothers:* in some ancient sources Charaxus is named as Sappho's elder
brother while Larichus is her younger. See notes on Nos. 80 (5*LP*) and 81
(15b*LP*).

[ι] *King of Olympus:* Zeus.

122

('CYPRIS SONG')[†]

How could anyone not have their heart broken
many times, Cypris – I mean by whomever
we truly love – and not wish to be set free
from pain? What do you

want of me when you cruelly tear me apart,
when you shake me with desire that saps the strength
from my limbs . . . ?[‡]

     . . . I wish you...
. . . might suffer this [torment too] . . .
               . . . I myself
know it [to be true] . . . .[§]

*****

[†] On Cypris (sometimes 'Kypris'), or Aphrodite, see also Section VI.
[‡] For an echo of these images see also Nos.1 (47*LP*) and 2 (130*LP*).
[§] These lines, with a then conjectural reading, previously formed No.29 (26*LP*). See 'The New Fragments: Texts, Translations and Retranslations'.

. . . [hurry now,] they are calling for us...
you have everything [we might need,] don't you
dear mother, for the festival . . .†

to celebrate its splendour in the spring? This
brings joy to mortals whose life is short. May I
[sing my songs] for so long as [I might have breath]
[and you want] to hear . . .

*****

† *festival:* thought to be that of Hera, held on Lesbos. See 'The New Fragments: Texts, Translations and Retranslations'.

124†

No, it is not possible for anyone
to be completely happy. And so we pray
that we might have our own small share. I myself
bear witness to this . . .

[seize the fleeting moment as it] comes to pass...
. . . you went away on the brink [of spring] . . . .‡
. . . [vanished like the melting] snow. But she . . .
. . . many things . . . .

*****

125[†]

. . . to speak [these words] . . .

. . . my tongue . . .

. . . forges fierce tales . . .[‡]

*****

126[§]

. . . without the passing seasons

night and [day would be as one] . . .

under a myriad stars

let us drink . . .

*****

[†] Previously known from the very damaged Oxyrhynchus papyrus, P.Oxy 1231 (18*LP*). The most readable part of the text offers the left-hand side of a poem in which, as in other fragments, the poet appears to celebrate her poetic art. See also Section VIII.

[‡] See also No. 89 (188LP)

[§] This is a previously unknown fragment.

Near here, lady Hera, we will celebrate
your treasured festival which the Atridai[‡]
themselves once established by a sacred vow,
illustrious kings,

after they had first suffered many ordeals
at Troy. Later they were beached here, on Lesbos,
for they could not find a path, could not complete
their own passage home

until they had given you their offerings
and to Zeus, suppliants' god, and Thyone's
entrancing son, Dionysus. Now we hold
those same rites of old,

sacred and [sublime]. And so [today] a throng
of young girls and married woman [have gathered]
around [your shrine . . .]

*****

† This is a new version of No.91 (17*LP*)
‡ *Atridae:* Agamemnon and Menelaus.

128[†]

The gifts of the Muses are violet-threaded,
rare: follow their path, my daughters, pursue
the lyre's clear-voiced, enthralling song.
Once I, too, was in tender bud. Now old age
is wrinkling my skin and my hair is turning
from black to grey; my heart is weighted,
knees buckle where I danced like a deer.
Yet what else can I do but complain?
To be human is to grow old. They say
Eös, the rosy-fingered dawn, whispered
of love to Tithonus, whirled him away
to the very edge of the world, beguiled
by his youth and beauty. Yet still he aged,
still he withered, despite his immortal wife.

*****

[†] This is a new version of No.31 (58*LP*). See 'The New Fragments: Texts, Translations and Retranslations'.

GLOSSARY

Acheron, one of the rivers of the lower world of the dead.

Achilles, son of Peleus and Thetis, one of the commanders of the Greek forces at Troy and the hero of the Iliad.

Actaeon, a keen huntsman, he spied on the goddess Artemis while she was bathing naked in a pool and was turned by her into a stag and torn to pieces by his own hounds.

Adonis, a beautiful youth loved by Aphrodite. He was killed, while hunting, by a boar. Aphrodite persuaded Zeus, the king of the gods, to restore him to life but Persephone, the queen of the lower world, who was also in love with him, refused to let him go. Zeus decreed that he should spend half the year in the lower world and the other half on earth. A fertility cult, popular with women, was associated with his death and rebirth, first in the East and then in Greece.

Aegean sea, between Greece and Asia Minor.

Alyattes, king of Lydia *c*.610-560 B.C., founder of the Lydian Empire.

Amorgos, small island in the Aegean, home of the poet Semonides.

Andromache, daughter of Eëtion, king of Thebe (Cilicia) and wife of Hector, prince of Troy.

Aphrodite, goddess of love and beauty, she sprang from the foam of the sea near Paphos in Cyprus or on the shore of Cythera, an Aegean island, hence her names, Cypris, Cytherea and Cyprogeneia (Cyprus-born).

Apollo, son of Leto and Zeus, sister of Artemis, god of music, archery, prophecy, medicine and youth. He was also associated with the sun and in Greek art was portrayed as the epitome of youthful male beauty. See note on No.97.

Ares, god of war.

Artemis, daughter of Leto and Zeus, sister of Apollo, a virgin moon goddess who had many aspects but was particularly associated with animals and wild places. See note on No. 97.

Asia Minor, modern Turkey.

Atridae, the brothers, Menelaus and Agamemnon, sons of Atreus, king of Mycenae. Menelaus married Helen and became king of Sparta, while Agamemnon married her sister, Clytemnestra. When Helen was abducted by Paris, Prince of Troy, they raised a Greek army to besiege the city with Agamemnon as its commander-in-chief. See notes on No.91 and No.127.

Charaxus, according to some ancient biographers, Sappho's brother and a wine-merchant. See notes on Nos. 80, 81 and 121.

Chiron, a centaur (half-man, half-horse), tutor to Achilles.

Cleanactidae, aristocratic family faction in Mytilene during Sappho's lifetime, of which the tyrant Myrsilus was a member.

Cleis, Sappho's daughter and, according to some sources, also the name of her mother.

Crete, island in the south Aegean, associated with the worship of Aphrodite.

Cypris, see **Aphrodite.**

Cyprus, the island in the eastern Mediterranean, the birthplace and haunt of Aphrodite.

Cytherea, see **Aphrodite.**

Dionysus, son of Semele, or Thyone, and Zeus and the god of the vine, fertility and poetry.

Eös, the dawn, lover of Tithonus. See notes on Nos. 91 and 128.

Eros, god of sexual desire, the attendant of Aphrodite.

Graces, companions of Aphrodite, three goddesses of beauty and charm.

Hades, god of death, king of the lower world.

Hector, prince of Troy, son of Priam and husband of Andromache.

Helen of Troy, queen of Sparta, wife of Menelaus and famous for her great beauty. In the *Iliad*, her abduction by Paris, prince of Troy, starts the war between Greece and Troy. After a ten-year siege of the city, she is recaptured by the victorious Greeks and returns to Sparta.

Hera, queen of the gods and Zeus' consort, she represents women, their lives, sexuality and occupations and was particularly worshipped on Lesbos. See note on Nos. 91, 123 and 127.

Hermes, messenger of the gods who conducts the souls of the dead to the lower world.

Hermione, daughter of Menelaus and Helen.

Hesperus, the evening star, depicted in Greek art as a young boy carrying a torch.

Idaeus, a stock name for Trojans in classical literature. In No.72, Idaeus is the name of the messenger who announces the arrival of Hector and Andromache at Troy.

Iliad, epic poem, attributed to Homer and probably composed in the eighth century B.C., which relates incidents of the Trojan War.

Ilus, the founder of Troy or Ilium. Trojans are sometimes referred to in literature as the sons or daughters of Ilus. See note on No.72.

Larichus, the younger brother of Sappho. See note on No. 121.

Leda, mother of Helen. See note on No.96.

Lesbos, island in the eastern Aegean, off the coast of Asia Minor, home of Sappho.

Leto, mother of Apollo and Artemis. See note on No.97.

Lydia, a rich and powerful kingdom of Asia Minor.

Menelaus, king of Sparta and husband of Helen. See notes on Nos. 91 and 127.

Muses, nine goddesses of literature, music and dance, connected with poetic inspiration.

Myrsilus, member of the Cleanactidae, one of the feuding aristocratic factions in Mytilene during Sappho's lifetime. He became tyrant of Mytilene in the early sixth century B.C.

Naucratis, port of the Nile delta, centre of contact between Greece and Egypt. See note on No.81.

Nereids, sea-nymphs, daughters of Nereus, the sea-god.

Niobe, turned to stone after her children were killed by Apollo and Artemis. See note on No.97.

Odysseus, king of Ithaca, a small island off the west coast of Greece and one of the Greek leaders at Troy, famous for his cunning.

Odyssey, epic poem attributed to Homer, probably composed in the eighth century B.C. It relates the ten-year adventures of Odysseus as he journeys home from Troy to Ithaca.

Paean, a hymn addressed to Apollo. In No.72 Sappho refers to Apollo himself as Paean.

Pandora, in Hesiod's poetry, the first woman on earth, created by Zeus as a punishment for the theft of fire by the demi-god, Prometheus. Pandora brought with her a box which she was forbidden to open but, overcome by curiosity, she did so and released all the evils of the world, trapping Hope inside when she quickly replaced the lid. According to Hesiod, Pandora and all other members of her sex are responsible for man's sufferings.

Panormus, a city mentioned in No.82 as a haunt of Aphrodite; its location is unknown for certain but is probably modern Palermo in Sicily.

Paphos, a town near the coast of southern Cyprus, reputed to be the place where Aphrodite emerged from the foam of the sea and famous as a centre for her worship.

Paris, prince of Troy, brother of Hector, son of Priam. In the *Iliad*, his abduction of Helen from Sparta to Troy causes the war between Greece and Troy.

Peleus, husband of the sea-nymph, Thetis, and the father of the Greek hero, Achilles.

Penelope, queen of Ithaca and wife of Odysseus. In the *Odyssey*, she rules Ithaca in his absence at Troy and is wooed by several suitors but remains faithful to Odysseus and waits patiently for his return.

Penthilidae, one of the rival families in Mytilene during Sappho's time, who claimed that they were the descendants of the mythical hero, Penthilus. In No.46, Sappho mentions them with disapproval.

Phaon, a legendary boatman of Lesbos, said by some ancient sources to be the subject of Sappho's unrequited love.

Pieria, a district of northern Greece, birthplace of the Muses.

Pittacus, of Mytilene *c*.650-570 B.C. He commanded the army in the war against Athenian colonists at Sigeum and killed the enemy leader in mortal combat. With Alcaeus, he was involved in a plot to overthrow the tyrant, Myrsilus, but changed sides, betrayed his companions and later became a tyrant himself.

Placia, river near Thebe in Cilicia, a district of southern Asia Minor.

Polyanactidae, aristocratic faction in Mytilene. See note on No.45.

Priam, father of Hector and king of Troy during the Trojan War. See note on No.72.

Rhodopis, courtesan of Naucratis, loved by Sappho's brother, Charaxus, and associated by Strabo with Doricha. See note on No.81.

Sardis, chief city of Lydia.

Sicyon, Greek city in the Peloponnese, home of the woman poet Praxilla.

Sigeum, promontory near Troy, colonised by Athenians *c*.600 B.C. and the subject of a war between Athens and Lesbos who both claimed territorial rights.

Socrates, Greek philosopher who lived in Athens 469-399 B.C. He taught philosophy to a group of young men, including Plato whose dialogues feature Socrates and his teachings. He was executed in 399 B.C. after being found guilty of two charges – religious unorthodoxy and corrupting the youth of the city.

Sparta, Greek city in the Peloponnese, in mythology ruled by Menelaus and Helen.

Thebe, city in Cilicia, a district of southern Asia Minor.

Thera, Greek island in the southern Aegean.

Thetis, sea-nymph, daughter of Nereus the god of the sea. She was married to Peleus and had a son, Achilles, the Greek hero of the Trojan War.

Thyone, or Semele, mother of the god Dionysus.

Tithonus, the mortal lover of Eös, the dawn. See notes on Nos. 31 and 128.

Troy, city in northern Asia Minor. In the *Iliad*, it is besieged by a Greek army for ten years and then destroyed by them in revenge for the abduction of Helen from Sparta by Paris.

Zeus, king of the gods.

Ancient Writers and Sources Mentioned in the Text

Aelian, rhetorician and writer. *c.* A.D. 170-235.

Alcaeus, lyric poet of Mytilene, contemporary of Sappho, *c.* 620-580 B.C.

Anacreon, lyric poet, *c.* 575-490 B.C.

Aristophanes, comic playwright, *c.* 450-385 B.C.

Aristotle, philosopher, 384-322 B.C.

Athenaeus, writer and anthologist, *fl. c.* A.D. 200.

Corinna, woman lyric poet, possibly fifth century B.C.

Dioscorides, epigrammatist, *fl.* 230 B.C.

Eusebius, Christian historian, *c.* A.D. 260-340.

Herodotus, historian, fifth century B.C.

Hesiod, epic poet, *c.* 700 B.C.

Homer, name given by the Greeks to the author of the epic poems, the *Iliad* and the *Odyssey*, although it is not even known whether they have a joint authorship. They were probably composed in the eighth century B.C. and reached their final form *c.* 700 B.C.

Horace, Roman poet, 65-08 B.C.

Maximus of Tyre, philosopher and rhetorician, *c.* A.D. 125-185.

Myrtis, woman lyric poet, fifth century B.C.

Ovid, Roman poet, 43 B.C.-A.D.17.

Palatine Anthology, compiled *c.* A.D. 980 of ealier Greek epigrams.

Parian Marble, a stone slab inscribed with a summary of Greek history up to 264/3 B.C.

Pausanias, traveller and geographer, *fl. c.* A.D. 150.

Philostratus, philosopher and writer, *c.* A.D. 170-247.

Pindar, choral lyric poet, 518-438 B.C.

Plato, philosopher, *c.* 429-347 B.C.

Plutarch, biographer, moralist and essayist, first century A.D.

Pollux, lexicographer and rhetorician, second century A.D.

Porphyrion, commentator on Horace, third century A.D.

Praxilla, lyric woman poet, *fl.* 451 B.C.

Semonides, iambic and elegiac poet, mid-seventh century B.C.

Solon, Athenian poet and statesman, *c.* 600 B.C.

Stobaeus, anthologist, early fifth century A.D.

Suda, an encyclopaedia, compiled in the tenth century A.D.

Zenobius, rhetorician, second century A.D.

Sappho's Companions

Anactoria:	*No.*21		Gongyla:	22, 30
Andromeda:	34, 42		Gorgo:	44, 45, 47
Archeanassa:	47		Gyrinno:	17
Atthis:	18, 33, 34, 35		Irana:	43
Dicca:	16		Micca:	46
Doricha:	81		Mnasidica:	17

CHRONOLOGICAL TABLE

Date	Event	Literature
776 B.C.	First Olympic Games.	
750		Homer
		Semonides
700		Hesiod
687	Kingdom of Lydia founded by Gyges.	
655-585	Tyranny at Corinth	
620-570	Tyranny at Mytilene: Pittacus, Alcaeus, Myrsilus.	Sappho and Alcaeus
610	War between Lesbos and Athenian colonists at Sigeum.	
610-560	Alyattes king of Lydia.	
595	Earliest Greek coins minted.	
594/3	Solon codifies Athenian law and makes constitutional reforms which lay down the foundation of the democratic state.	Solon
582-573	Pythian, Isthmian and Nemean Games established.	
572	Marriage contest for Agariste, daughter of Cleisthenes, tyrant of Sicyon.	
561-510	Tyranny at Athens.	
		Anacreon
508/7	Cleisthenes makes further democratic reforms at Athens.	
		Myrtis
		Corinna
		Pindar
490	First Persian expedition against Greece defeated at the battle of Marathon.	
480/79	Second Persian invasion, again defeated.	Herodotus
461	Ephialtes makes radical democratic reforms at Athens.	Tragedy at Athens: Aeschylus Sophocles Euripides
451	Pericles' law at Athens restricting citizenship to men whose parents are both Athenian.	Praxilla
431-404	Second Peloponnesian War between Athens and Sparta.	Aristophanes

Date	Event	Literature
411-410 and 404	Right-wing revolutions at Athens overthrow the democracy and establish an oligarchy.	Plato
399	Socrates executed at Athens by the restored democracy.	
343	Aristotle at Macedon as tutor to Alexander.	Aristotle
338	Athens defeated by Philip of Macedon.	
336	Alexander becomes king of Macedon.	

KEY TO THE FRAGMENTS: 1

Translations	LP	Translations	LP	Translations	LP	Translations	LP
1	47	31	58	61	109	91	17
2	130	32	94	62	112	92	154
3	138	33	96	63	113	93	1.a. 16
4	46	34	131	64	115	94	168
5	i.a. 25	35	49	65	111	95	140a
6	147	36	129	66	110a	96	166
7	146	37	57	67	116 & 117	97	142
8	52	38	976*PMG*	68	105a & c	98	160
9	145	39	137	69	107	99	118
10	120	40	102	70	152*E*	100	1a*E*
11	41	41	121	71	114	101	106
12	126	42	133	72	44	102	128
13	149 & 151	43	91	73	141	103	53
14	23	44	144	74	98a & b	104	127
15	56	45	155	75	132	105	32
16	81b	46	71 *ll*.1-3	76	150	106	193
17	82a	47	213 *ll*.1-2	77	122	107	55
18	8	48	51	78	1	108	43 *ll*.8-9
19	i.a. 13	49	36	79	2	109	104b
20	31	50	37	80	5	110	104a
21	16	51	38	81	15b	111	34
22	22	52	45	82	35	112	34
23	156 & 167	53	24a *ll*.2-4	83	33	113	143
24	100	54	125	84	40	114	136
25	39	55	185 & 153	85	133b	115	42
26	48	56	21 *ll*.11-13	86	134	116	201
27	197	57	i.a. 26	87	159	117	204
28	123	58	27 1.8	88	54	118	158
29	26 *ll*.2-4	59	30	89	172 & 188	119	50
30	95	60	108	90	200; 90; 33*E*	120	148

LP = Lobel & Page

KEY TO THE FRAGMENTS: 2

LP	Translations	LP	Translations	LP	Translations	LP	Translations
1	78	49	35	114	71	148	120
2	79	50	119	115	64	149	13
5	80	51	48	116	67	150	76
8	18	52	8	117	67	151	13
15b	81	53	103	118	99	153	55
16	21	54	88	120	10	154	92
17	91	55	107	121	41	155	45
21 *ll*.11-13	56	56	15	122	77	156	23
22	22	57	37	123	28	158	118
23	14	58	31	125	54	159	87
24a *ll*.2-4	53	71 *ll*.1-3	46	126	12	160	98
26 *ll*.2-4	29	81b	16	127	104	166	96
27 1.8	58	82a	17	128	102	167	23
30	59	90	90	129	36	168	94
31	20	91	43	130	2	172	89
32	105	94	32	131	34	185	55
33	83	95	30	132	75	188	89
34	111 & 112	96	33	133	42 & 85	193	106
35	82	98a & b	74	134	86	197	27
36	49	100	24	136	114	200	90
37	50	102	40	137	39	201	116
38	51	104a	110	138	3	204	117
39	25	104c	109	140a	95	213 *ll*.1-2	47
40	84	105a & c	68	141	73	i.a. 13	19
41	11	106	101	142	97	i.a. 16	93
42	115	107	69	143	113	i.a. 25	5
43 *ll*.8-9	108	108	60	144	44	i.a. 26	57
44	72	109	61	145	9	1a*E*	100
45	52	110a	66	146	7	33*E*	90
46	4	111	65	147	6	152*E*	70
47	1	112	62			976*PMG*	38
48	26	113	63				

KEY TO THE NEW FRAGMENTS

Translations	Text
21	'fragment 16' (P.GC inv.105 fr.2 + 16LP))
80	'fragment 5' (P.GC inv.105 fr.3 + 5LP)
121	'Brothers Poem' (P. Sapph.Obbink)
122	'Cypris Song' (P.Sapph.Obbink)
123	'fragment 9' (P.GC inv.105 fr.1 + 9LP)
124	'fragment 16a' (P.GC inv.105 fr.2 + 16 & 26LP)
125	'fragment 18' (P.GC inv.105 fr.3 + 18LP)
126	'fragment 18a' (P.GC inv.105 fr. 3)
127	'fragment 17' (P.GC inv.105 fr.2 + 17LP)
128	'Cologne fragment' (*P.Köln* inv. 21351 & 21376 + 58LP)

Text	Translations
'fragment 5'	80
'fragment 9'	123
'fragment 16'	21
'fragment 16a'	124
'fragment 17'	127
'fragment 18'	125
'fragment 18a'	126
'Brothers Poem'	121
'Cypris Song'	122
'Cologne fragment'	128

Abbreviations:
P.GC = Green Collection, Oklahoma City
P. Sapph. Obbink = privately owned papyrus (formerly Robinson Collection, University of Mississippi, USA)
P.Köln = Cologne Papyrus Collection
LP = Lobel & Page

SELECT BIBLIOGRAPHY

Marilyn Arthur (1977): 'Liberated Women: The Classical Era', in R. Bridenthal and C. Koonz , 60-89.

Josephine Balmer (1996): *Classical Women Poets* (Newcastle upon Tyne: Bloodaxe Books).

———————— (2013) *Piecing Together The Fragments: Translating Classical Verse, Creating Contemporary Poetry* (Oxford: Oxford University Press).

Silvio Bär (2016): 'Ceci n'est pas un fragment: Identity, Intertextuality and Fictionality in Sappho's Brothers Poem', *Symbolae Osloenses*, 90, 8-54.

Willis Barnstone (1962): *Greek Lyric Poetry* (New York: Bantam Books).

Anton Bierl and **André Lardinois** (eds.) (2016): *The Newest Sappho: P. Sapph. Obbink and P. GC inv. 105, frs.1–4.* (Leiden: Brill).

John Boardman and **E. La Rocca** (1978): *Eros in Greece* (London: Phaidon).

Ewen Bowie (2016): 'How Did Sappho's Songs Get into the Male Sympotic Repertoire?', in Bierl and Lardinois, 148-164.

C.M. Bowra (1961): *Greek Lyric Poetry*, 2nd ed. (Oxford: Oxford University Press).

R. Bridenthal and **C. Koonz** (eds.) (1977): *Becoming Visible: Women in European History* (Boston: Houghton Mifflin).

A.R. Burn (1978): *The Lyric Age of Greece* (London: Edward Arnold).

S. Burris, J. Fish and **D. Obbink** (2014): 'New Fragments of Book 1 of Sappho', *Zeitschrift für Papyrologie und Epigraphik*, 189, 1-28.

David A. Campbell (1976): (ed.) *Greek Lyric Poetry* (London: Macmillan).

———————— (1982): (ed.) *Greek Lyric 1* (London: Loeb Classical Library).

———————— (1983): *The Golden Lyre: The Themes of the Greek Lyric Poets* (London: Duckworth).

J.A. Davison (1968): *From Archilochus to Pindar* (London: Macmillan).

George Devereux (1970): 'The Nature of Sappho's Seizure in fr. 31*LP* as Evidence of her Inversion', *Classical Quarterly* n.s. 20, 17-31.

K.J. Dover (1978): *Greek Homosexuality* (London: Duckworth).

Page duBois (1978): 'Sappho and Helen', *Arethusa* 11, 89-99.

———————— (1995), *Sappho is Burning* (Chicago: University of Chicago Press).

H. Fränkel (1975): *Early Greek Poetry and Philosophy*, trans. M. Hadas and J.Willis (Oxford: Blackwell).

Ellen Greene (ed.) (1996a): *Reading Sappho: Contemporary Approaches* (Berkeley and London: University of California Press).

————— (ed.) (1996b): *Re-reading Sappho: Reception and Transmission* (Berkeley and London: University of California Press).

B.P. Grenfell and A.S. Hunt (1898): *Oxyrhynchus Papyri I* (London: Egypt Exploration Fund).

Judith Hallett (1979): 'Sappho and her Social Context: Sense and Sensuality', *Signs*, 4, 447-64.

Richard Jenkyns (1982): *Three Classical Poets: Sappho, Catullus and Juvenal* (London: Duckworth).

Hugh Kenner (1971): *The Pound Era* (Berkeley & London : University of California Press).

Leslie Kurke (2016): 'Gendered Spheres and Mythic Models in Sappho's Brothers Poem'. In Bierl and Lardinois, 238-265.

André Lardinois (2016): 'Sappho's Brothers Song and the Fictionality of Early Greek Lyric Poetry,' in Bierl and Lardinois, 167-187.

Mary R. Lefkowitz (1981): *Heroines and Hysterics* (London: Duckworth).

Mary R. Lefkowitz and Maureen B. Fant (eds) (1982): *Women's Life in Greece and Rome: A Source Book in Translation* (London: Duckworth).

Albin Lesky (1966): *A History of Greek Literature*, trans. J.Willis and C. de Heer (London: Methuen).

Joel Lidov (2016): 'Songs for Sailors and Lovers', in Bierl and Lardinois, 55-109.

Edgar Lobel and Denys Page (eds.) (1955): *Poetarum Lesbiorum Fragmenta* (Oxford: Oxford University Press).

Thomas McEvilley (1971): 'Sappho, fragment ninety-four', *Phoenix* 25, 1-11.

M. Marcovich (1972): 'Sappho fr.31: anxiety attack or love declaration?', *Classical Quarterly*, n.s. 22, 19-32.

John D. Marry (1979): 'Sappho and the heroic ideal: *erotos arete*', *Arethusa*, 12, 71-92.

Melissa Mueller (2016): 'Re-Centering Epic *Nostos*: Gender and Genre in Sappho's Brothers Poem', *Arethusa*, 49 (1) 25-46.

Oswyn Murray (1980): *Early Greece* (London: Fontana).

Dirk Obbink (2014): 'Two New Poems by Sappho', *Zeitschrift für Papyrologie und Epigraphik*, 189, 32-49.

————— (2015): 'Interim Notes on "Two New Poems by Sappho"', *Zeitschrift für Papyrologie und Epigraphik*, 194, 1-8.

————— (2016a): 'The Newest Sappho: Text, Apparatus Criticus, and Translation', in Bierl and Lardinois, 13-33.

—————— (2016b): 'Ten New Poems of Sappho: Provenance, Authenticity and Text of the New Sappho Papyri', in Bierl and Lardinois, 34-54.

—————— (2016c): 'Goodbye Family Gloom! The Coming of Charaxos in the Brothers Song,' in Bierl and Lardinois, 208-224.

Denys Page (1955): *Sappho and Alcaeus* (Oxford: Oxford University Press).

Sarah Pomeroy (1975): *Goddesses, Whores, Wives and Slaves: Women in Classical Antiquity* (New York: Schocken Books).

Diane Rayor (2016): 'Reimagining the Fragments of Sappho through Translation', in Bierl and Lardinois, 396-412.

Diane Rayor and **André Lardinois** (2014): *Sappho: A New Translation of the Complete Works* (Cambridge: Cambridge University Press).

Margaret Reynolds (ed.) (2000): *The Sappho Companion* (London: Chatto & Windus).

David M. Robinson (1925): *Sappho and her Influence* (London: Harrap).

Jane M. Snyder (1989), *The Woman and the Lyre: Women Writers in Classical Greece and Rome* (Bristol: Bristol Classical Press).

Eva Stehle (2016): 'Larichos in the Brothers Poem: Sappho Speaks Truth to the Wine-Pourer,' in Bierl and Lardinois, 266-292.

Odysseus Tsagarakis (1977): *Self-expression in Early Greek Lyric, Elegiac and Iambic Poetry* (Wiesbaden: Steiner, 1977).

M.L. West (2005): 'The New Sappho,' *Zeitschrift für Papyrologie und Epigraphik*, 151, 1–9.

—————— (2014), 'Nine poems of Sappho', *Zeitschrift für Papyrologie und Epigraphik*, 191, 1–12.

Ulrich von Wilamowitz-Moellendorff (1913): *Sappho und Simonides* (Berlin: Weidmann).

Margaret Williamson (1995): *Sappho's Immortal Daughters* (Cambridge, Massachusetts and London: Harvard University Press).

F.A. Wright (1923): 'The Women Poets of Greece', *Fortnightly Review*, 113 (February 1923), 323-33.

Classical Women Poets

translated by **JOSEPHINE BALMER**

Fragmented and forgotten, the women poets of ancient Greece and Rome have long been overlooked by translators and scholars. Yet to Antipater of Thessalonica, writing in the first century AD, these were the 'earthly Muses' whose poetic skills rivalled those of their heavenly namesakes: 'Their songs delight the gods...and mortals too for all time.' Today only a fraction of their work survives – lyrical, witty, often innovative, and always moving – offering surprising insights into the closed world of women in antiquity, from childhood friendships through love affairs and marriage to motherhood and bereavement. Josephine Balmer's translations breathe new life into long-lost works by over a dozen poets from early Greece to the late Roman empire, including Sappho, Corinna, Erinna and Sulpicia, as well as inscriptions, folk-songs and even graffiti. Each poet is introduced by a brief bibliographical note, and where necessary unfamiliar mythological or historical references are explained. *Classical Women Poets* is a companion volume to Josephine Balmer's edition *Sappho: Poems & Fragments*, also published by Bloodaxe.

Printed in the USA
CPSIA information can be obtained
at www.ICGtesting.com
JSHW082213140824
68134JS00014B/604